TRAUMA-FOCUSED

ACT

for Adults

A Guide to Implementing TF-ACT's Major Principles for Effectively Managing Painful Thoughts and Experiences to Regain Control of Your Life

Alice Glover

Trauma-Focused ACT

for Adults

A Guide to Implementing TF-ACT's Major Principles for
Effectively Managing Painful Thoughts and Experiences
to Regain Control of Your Life

Dr. ALICE GLOVER

Editorial Director:
Thomson Matthew
Cover Design:
James Benjamin
Editorial and Production Services:
Gospel Pen Publishers

Contents

FOREWORD ix

Introduction 1

Trauma-Focused Acceptance and Commitment
Therapy (ACT) 1

Chapter One 3

What You've Been Through 3

What Is Trauma? 5

Types of Trauma 8

How Trauma Affects the Brain and Body 10

The Link Between Trauma and Negative Thinking 13

Reframing Trauma as a Part of Your Life Story 15

Chapter Two 19

The Core Principles of ACT 19

Acceptance 22

Cognitive Defusion 24

Mindfulness 27

The Observing Self 30

Values 32

Committed Action... 35

Chapter 3 39

Acceptance – Letting Go of the Struggle
Against Pain 39

What Does It Mean to Accept Trauma? 41

Exercises for Practicing Acceptance............................47

Accepting Emotions without Judgment......................49

Chapter 4..**55**

Separating Yourself from Traumatic Thoughts 55

The Problem with Over-Identifying with Thoughts 60

Defusion Techniques for Traumatic Memories............62

Chapter 5..**69**

Allowing Space for Difficult Emotions........................69

Practical Techniques for Emotional Expansion 77

Balancing Emotional Expansion with Self-Care...........80

Chapter 6..**87**

Breaking Free from the Past..87

The Power of the Present Moment in Trauma
Recovery 89

Coping with Flashbacks and Intrusive Thoughts
in the Present 97

Chapter 7..**103**

The Observing Self – Cultivating a Balanced
Perspective on Trauma..103

What Is the Observing Self? 105

Techniques for Accessing the Observing Self.............110

Chapter Eight 119

Rediscovering What Truly Matters 119

The Role of Values in Trauma Recovery 122

Overcoming Barriers to Living a Values-Based Life ...129

Chapter 9 135

Committed Action – Moving Forward with Purpose . 135

Setting Goals for Trauma Recovery...............................139

Creating a Roadmap for Long-Term Action 146

Chapter 10 151

The Path Forward – Integrating Trauma-Focused ACT into Daily Life 151

Applying ACT Principles in Everyday Situations 154

Maintaining Long-Term Motivation and Growth 158

Navigating Setbacks with ACT Tools 161

Conclusion 167

Maintain Lasting Healing and Growth 167

FOREWORD

Trauma has a way of shaping lives in ways we never imagined, often pulling us away from the people we once were or hoped to become. It can leave us feeling trapped—bound by painful memories, distorted by fears, and overwhelmed by emotions we can't always name or understand. In moments like these, even the simplest tasks can feel insurmountable. We may begin to question our strength, our resilience, and our ability to move forward. But if there's one truth I've come to understand over years of working with trauma survivors, it's this: trauma does not define you. Your past experiences, no matter how painful, do not hold the final word on who you are or what your future holds. This book is about finding that future again, and more importantly, reclaiming your life with the help of a powerful tool: Acceptance and Commitment Therapy (ACT).

Acceptance and Commitment Therapy, or ACT, is not just a clinical method; it's a compassionate way of approaching the pain we all carry in some form. At its core, ACT doesn't demand that we erase our trauma or pretend it never happened. Instead, it asks us to hold space for it, to allow it to be part of our story without letting it dominate our narrative. It asks us to expand—to soften into our emotions rather than harden against them. This might sound counterintuitive at first, especially in a world that often tells us to fight our pain or "just get over it." But that's where the beauty of ACT lies: it doesn't rely on denial or repression, but rather on acceptance and action. It invites you to live a life aligned with your deepest values, even when pain and discomfort are present.

As you journey through the principles of Trauma-Focused ACT laid out in this book, you'll find that these concepts are not about rigid steps or one-size-fits-all solutions. Instead, they offer a framework—a way of thinking and being that empowers you to respond to life's challenges with flexibility, openness, and intention. Cognitive defusion, for example, helps you unhook from the mental loops that often keep you stuck in old patterns of thinking. It's not about silencing your thoughts, but learning to see them for what they are: temporary experiences, not truths that define your worth or potential. Expansion and acceptance, on the other hand, teach you to sit with difficult emotions without letting them consume you. These are not passive acts of surrender but powerful gestures of courage and self-compassion.

One of the most transformative aspects of ACT is its focus on the present moment. Trauma has a tendency to root us in the past or push us toward an anxious future. But ACT invites you to come back to where your true power lies: the here and now. Through mindfulness and present-moment awareness, you'll discover that even in the midst of pain, there is still beauty, still peace, still the possibility for connection and growth. It's about breaking free from the grip of autopilot living and truly engaging with your life as it is happening, no matter how imperfect or messy it may seem.

And then, there's the Observing Self—perhaps one of the most profound concepts you'll encounter in this book. This is the part of you that is untouched by trauma, the inner witness who can step back and see the unfolding of your life without judgment or attachment. It's the quiet voice inside that says, "You are more than your experiences, more than your pain." Tapping into this deeper part of yourself allows you to move through the world with greater clarity and calm, even in moments of distress.

But none of this works without knowing what truly matters to you. Values clarification, as you'll learn, is not just about lofty ideals or abstract goals. It's about asking yourself the hard questions: What do I want my life to stand for? What kind of person do I want to be, even in the face of hardship? And once you find your answers, ACT encourages you to take committed action—to make small, meaningful steps toward those values, no matter how difficult the path may seem.

This book isn't just a guide to understanding ACT; it's an invitation to step into the life you deserve. Each chapter will walk you through principles designed to help you move from a place of suffering and limitation to one of empowerment and freedom. It's not an easy road, but I promise you it's one worth taking. And as you begin this journey, know that you are not alone. You have the strength within you, and you have this framework to guide you.

Introduction

Trauma-Focused Acceptance and Commitment Therapy (ACT)

Trauma-focused Acceptance and Commitment Therapy (ACT) is a powerful therapeutic approach that blends the principles of ACT with the specific needs of trauma survivors. At its core, ACT encourages individuals to accept their painful emotions and thoughts rather than avoid or suppress them. For those who have experienced trauma, this is especially important, as the natural instinct is often to push away memories, flashbacks, or emotional pain. But this avoidance can make the distress even more intense over time. Trauma-focused ACT helps survivors break free from the cycle of avoidance and find a way to live more fully in the present, despite the lingering impact of past experiences.

What makes this approach particularly effective for trauma recovery is how it integrates mindfulness, acceptance, and committed action with the unique challenges trauma presents. By teaching individuals to develop psychological flexibility, ACT helps them recognize that while trauma-related thoughts and feelings are difficult, they don't have to dictate their lives. This therapy creates space for survivors to engage with their pain without being consumed by it, fostering emotional resilience. Rather than battling against triggers and flashbacks, survivors learn how to coexist with them, seeing these experiences as part of the broader human condition rather than signs of personal weakness.

The process of ACT involves learning to be present with discomfort while simultaneously identifying and pursuing meaningful life values. Trauma-focused ACT helps survivors find clarity about what truly matters to them, even in the midst of emotional upheaval. It empowers individuals to take concrete steps toward the life they want, despite the inevitable pain that arises from trauma. This approach is deeply compassionate, as it honors the trauma while also encouraging growth, helping individuals cultivate both self-compassion and strength as they navigate their healing journey.

With its focus on acceptance and mindful action, trauma-focused ACT provides a path forward that doesn't rely on erasing the past but instead focuses on moving through it. Survivors are not just taught how to manage their symptoms, but how to reshape their relationship with pain, allowing them to live with greater freedom and authenticity. This makes ACT a uniquely hopeful and practical approach for those seeking to heal and build a life grounded in resilience and purpose.

Chapter One

What You've Been Through

Trauma leaves invisible marks that shape who we are and how we move through the world. If you're reading this, you've likely carried those marks—perhaps for a long time—and I want to acknowledge the immense courage it takes to face the pain, the memories, and the effects of what you've been through. Trauma, in all its forms, isn't just a singular event locked away in the past. It can seep into the present, influencing the way you think, feel, and even the way your body responds to everyday experiences. It can alter your sense of safety, trust, and the way you connect with others. And while no two journeys through trauma are the same, one thing remains constant: the struggle to reclaim a sense of self that feels whole again.

This chapter is a space where we will take a closer look at trauma—not just as a concept, but as something that has shaped your life in profound and often confusing ways. I'm not here to tell you how you should feel about what happened to you. Instead, I want to create a safe space to explore how trauma affects both the mind and the body. You may have noticed changes in your behavior or emotions that seem inexplicable or even overwhelming. You might have difficulty focusing, sleeping, or even feeling connected to your own body. These are all natural responses to trauma, even if they sometimes make you feel disconnected from yourself or the world around you. Understanding these effects is not about justifying them, but about giving yourself permission to feel what you feel, knowing that you are not alone in these reactions.

What makes trauma particularly challenging is that its effects don't always announce themselves immediately or in ways that feel logical. Trauma can live quietly in the body, often manifesting in ways we don't fully recognize—through anxiety, chronic stress, or even physical pain. The mind, too, may become a battleground of intrusive thoughts, flashbacks, or feelings of numbness. We will discuss these layers of trauma in detail because understanding what's happening inside of you is a crucial first step toward healing. Trauma is not just an emotional wound; it is a whole-body experience that rewires how we function on multiple levels.

Before diving into the deeper healing process, it's important to grasp the full scope of trauma's impact. Sometimes, the more we try to "push through" without fully understanding what we're working against, the more stuck we feel. This chapter will guide you through that understanding, helping you to recognize that your reactions, your emotions, and your challenges are not signs of weakness, but rather evidence of your strength in surviving. By acknowledging what trauma truly is, we open the door to beginning the process of healing in a more meaningful, compassionate way.

We're not here to rush through this process or to minimize the complexities of what you've been through. Instead, we will begin with understanding—because only when we fully understand trauma can we begin to loosen its grip on our lives. As we explore these ideas together, know that there is no judgment here, only empathy.

What Is Trauma?

Trauma is a profound and often life-altering experience that can touch anyone, regardless of age, background, or culture. At its core, trauma is a response to an event or series of events that overwhelm a person's ability to cope, leaving them feeling helpless, frightened, and deeply affected. This can manifest in many forms, each with its own unique set of challenges and impacts.

Emotional trauma, for instance, often arises from experiences like the loss of a loved one, a significant betrayal, or a deeply distressing event. It can feel like a constant weight on your heart, making it hard to find joy or peace in daily life. Emotional trauma can lead to feelings of isolation, anxiety, and a sense of disconnection from the world around you. You might find yourself replaying the event over and over in your mind, struggling to make sense of what happened and why it feels so impossible to move on.

Physical trauma, on the other hand, is often the result of accidents, injuries, or acts of violence. The pain and discomfort can be immediate and intense, but the lasting effects can be just as significant. Physical trauma can leave scars, both visible and invisible, that remind you of the event long after the initial pain has subsided. It can also lead to chronic pain, fatigue, and a host of other physical symptoms that can make it difficult to function day to day. The body holds onto these memories, and even the smallest trigger can bring back the flood of emotions and sensations.

Sexual trauma, including experiences of sexual assault or abuse, is a particularly devastating form of trauma. It can shatter your sense of safety and trust, making it hard to feel secure in your own skin. The emotional and psychological impact can be profound, leading to symptoms like post-traumatic stress disorder (PTSD), depression, and anxiety. You might struggle with intimacy, self-esteem, and a sense of control over your own body. The trauma can feel like a constant shadow, always present, even when you try to push it away.

Trauma doesn't just affect the mind and emotions; it also has a significant impact on the body. When you experience trauma, your body's stress response system goes into overdrive. This can lead to a host of physiological changes, such as increased heart rate, heightened blood pressure, and a surge of stress hormones like cortisol and adrenaline. Over time, these changes can take a toll on your physical health, leading to issues like chronic pain, gastrointestinal problems, and even a weakened immune system. The body and mind are deeply interconnected, and trauma can disrupt this balance, making it hard to feel truly at ease.

One of the most challenging aspects of trauma is how it can affect your relationships and sense of self. You might find it hard to trust others, to open up, or to form deep connections. The world can feel like a dangerous place, and even the most mundane activities can feel fraught with risk. You might start to avoid certain places, people, or activities that remind you of the trauma, which can limit your life in significant ways. The trauma can also make it hard to see yourself clearly, leading to feelings of shame, guilt, and self-blame. You might wonder why you can't just "get over it" or why you feel so different from who you were before.

Despite the challenges, it's important to remember that healing is possible. Trauma can be a deeply isolating experience, but you are not alone. Many people have walked this path before you, and there are tools and resources available to help you regain control of your life. Trauma-Focused Acceptance and Commitment Therapy (TF-ACT) is one such approach that can help you navigate these challenges. By learning to accept your experiences, develop psychological flexibility, and reconnect with your values, you can begin to build a life that is meaningful and fulfilling, even in the face of trauma. The journey may be difficult, but it is also a journey of growth, resilience, and ultimately, healing.

Types of Trauma

When delving into the world of trauma, it's important to understand that not all traumatic experiences are created equal. Each type of trauma—acute, chronic, and complex—has its own unique characteristics and effects on individuals. By exploring these distinctions, we can better understand how to support those who have experienced trauma and guide them toward healing and resilience.

Acute trauma is often the result of a single, intense, and overwhelming event. This could be a car accident, a natural disaster, or a violent assault. The impact of acute trauma is immediate and can be profound. For example, imagine a person who has survived a severe car crash. In the aftermath, they might experience intense flashbacks, where the sound of a car engine or the sight of a similar vehicle can trigger a flood of distressing memories. They might also struggle with hypervigilance, constantly on edge and hyper-aware of their surroundings, as if another crash is just around the corner. Acute trauma can shatter a person's sense of safety and control, making it difficult to trust the world around them. However, with the right support and interventions, many individuals can recover and regain a sense of normalcy.

Chronic trauma, on the other hand, results from prolonged and repeated exposure to traumatic events. This type of trauma is often associated with ongoing abuse, such as emotional, physical, or sexual abuse, or living in a war zone. The effects of chronic trauma are cumulative and can deeply affect a person's psychological and emotional well-being. For instance, a child who grows up in a household with a verbally abusive parent might develop a chronic sense of worthlessness and self-doubt. They might struggle with forming healthy relationships, always anticipating rejection or criticism. Chronic trauma can create a persistent state of anxiety and fear, making it challenging to feel safe or secure. Over time, this can lead to a range of mental health issues, including depression, anxiety, and post-traumatic stress disorder (PTSD). Understanding the long-term impact of chronic trauma is crucial for providing the right kind of support and interventions that address the deep-seated issues that have developed over time.

Complex trauma is a particularly intricate form of trauma that arises from multiple, varied, and often interrelated traumatic experiences. These experiences are typically severe, prolonged, and interpersonal, involving repeated violations of trust and safety. For example, a person who has experienced both childhood abuse and later, as an adult, survived a violent assault, is likely to have complex trauma. The effects of complex trauma are multifaceted and can include difficulties with emotional regulation, attachment, and identity. Such individuals might struggle with intense feelings of shame and guilt, often believing that the trauma was their fault. They might also have fragmented memories and a distorted sense of self, making it challenging to form a coherent narrative of their life. Complex trauma can lead to a profound sense of disconnection from oneself and others, making it essential to approach healing with a holistic and compassionate perspective.

Each type of trauma—acute, chronic, and complex—has its own unique challenges and effects on individuals. Understanding these distinctions is crucial for providing the right kind of support and interventions. By recognizing the specific needs and experiences of those who have endured trauma, we can offer them the guidance and encouragement they need to navigate their healing journey. Whether it's the immediate impact of a single event, the cumulative effects of repeated exposure, or the multifaceted challenges of complex trauma, the path to recovery is possible with the right tools and support.

How Trauma Affects the Brain and Body

When we experience trauma, our brain and body undergo a series of complex and profound changes. These changes are designed to help us survive in the moment, but they can also leave lasting impacts that affect our mental and physical health over time. Understanding these effects can provide a foundation for healing and regaining control over our lives.

At the core of our response to trauma is the fight, flight, or freeze response, an ancient survival mechanism hardwired into our brains. When we encounter a threat, our brain quickly assesses the situation and decides on the best course of action. This decision is made in the amygdala, a small, almond-shaped structure deep within the brain that is responsible for processing emotions, especially fear. The amygdala sends signals to the hypothalamus, which then triggers the release of stress hormones like cortisol and adrenaline. These hormones prepare our body for action by increasing heart rate, elevating blood pressure, and flooding our muscles with glucose for energy. This is the fight or flight response, where we either confront the threat head-on or flee to safety.

However, in some cases, the threat is so overwhelming that neither fighting nor fleeing seems like a viable option. In these instances, our brain may opt for the freeze response, a state of immobilization where the body becomes temporarily paralyzed. This response can be seen in animals that "play dead" when faced with a predator, and it serves a similar purpose in humans—by appearing non-threatening, we may avoid further harm.

While these responses are crucial in the moment, they can have long-term effects when trauma is severe or repeated. One of the most well-known long-term consequences of trauma is Post-Traumatic Stress Disorder (PTSD). PTSD occurs when the brain remains in a heightened state of alert, even when the threat is no longer present. This persistent state of arousal can lead to a range of symptoms, including hypervigilance, where individuals are constantly on edge, scanning their environment for potential threats. This heightened vigilance can be exhausting and make it difficult to relax or feel safe.

Another common symptom of PTSD is anxiety, which can manifest as excessive worry, fear, and a sense of impending doom. This anxiety is often rooted in the brain's continued release of stress hormones, which can disrupt the functioning of other brain regions, such as the prefrontal cortex, which is responsible for rational thinking and decision-making. As a result, individuals with PTSD may find it challenging to manage their emotions and make clear-headed decisions.

Trauma can also affect the structure and function of the brain. For example, chronic stress can lead to the shrinkage of the hippocampus, a region involved in memory and learning. This can result in difficulties with memory and concentration, making it harder to form new memories or recall past events. Additionally, the amygdala, which is already overactive in individuals with PTSD, can become even more sensitive, leading to heightened emotional reactions to stimuli that might not have been threatening before.

The body, too, is not immune to the effects of trauma. Chronic stress can weaken the immune system, making individuals more susceptible to illness and disease. It can also lead to chronic pain, as the body remains in a state of tension and inflammation. Over time, these physical symptoms can further exacerbate mental health issues, creating a vicious cycle that can be challenging to break.

Understanding these neurological and physiological effects is crucial for anyone seeking to heal from trauma. By recognizing how trauma impacts the brain and body, we can begin to develop strategies to counteract these effects and regain a sense of control and well-being. This journey involves learning to manage our stress response, retraining our brain to respond more adaptively, and finding ways to soothe our body's physical symptoms.

With the right tools and support, it is possible to move beyond the grip of trauma and live a more fulfilling, meaningful life.

The Link Between Trauma and Negative Thinking

Trauma has a profound and often lasting impact on the way we think and perceive the world around us. When we experience trauma, our brains and bodies go into a heightened state of alert, designed to protect us from further harm. This survival mechanism is incredibly powerful, but it can also leave us with persistent negative thinking patterns that can be challenging to break. These patterns, such as self-blame, catastrophizing, and hopelessness, are not just random thoughts; they are deeply rooted in the psychological mechanisms that our minds use to process and cope with trauma.

Self-blame is a common response to trauma, and it often stems from a deep-seated need to make sense of what has happened. When something traumatic occurs, our brains try to find a reason or a cause, and sometimes, the easiest target is ourselves. We might think, "If only I had done something differently, this wouldn't have happened." This self-blame can be a way of maintaining a sense of control in a situation where we felt utterly powerless. However, it can also lead to a cycle of guilt and shame, making it difficult to move forward. It's important to recognize that trauma is not your fault, and that the responsibility for what happened lies with the perpetrator or the circumstances, not with you. By understanding this, you can begin to shift the focus from self-blame to self-compassion.

Catastrophizing is another common pattern that emerges after trauma. It involves consistently expecting the worst possible outcome in any given situation. For example, you might find yourself thinking, "If I go to that party, something terrible will happen," or "If I try to get a new job, I'll fail and end up feeling even worse." This type of thinking is a way for your brain to prepare for potential threats, but it can also create a self-fulfilling prophecy. When you expect the worst, you might avoid taking risks or engaging in activities that could be beneficial, which can lead to a sense of isolation and stagnation. Recognizing that catastrophizing is a protective mechanism can help you challenge these thoughts. By asking yourself, "What evidence do I have that this will happen?" or "What's the best possible outcome?" you can begin to broaden your perspective and open yourself up to new possibilities.

Hopelessness is perhaps one of the most debilitating consequences of trauma. It can manifest as a deep belief that things will never get better, that you are stuck in your current situation, and that there is no way out. This feeling of hopelessness is often fueled by the persistent negative thoughts and emotions that follow trauma. When you feel hopeless, it can be difficult to see a way forward, and you might find yourself giving up on things that could bring you joy or fulfillment. However, it's important to remember that hopelessness is not a permanent state. It is a feeling that can be changed, and there are steps you can take to regain a sense of hope. One powerful tool is to focus on small, achievable goals. By setting and accomplishing these goals, you can build momentum and gradually shift your perspective. Additionally, connecting with others who understand what you're going through can provide a sense of support and validation, helping you to see that you are not alone in your struggles.

Understanding the psychological mechanisms behind these negative thinking patterns is the first step in breaking free from their hold. Trauma can feel like a dark cloud that looms over every aspect of your life, but it's important to remember that you have the power to change your thoughts and, in turn, your emotional experience. By recognizing and challenging these patterns, you can begin to reclaim your sense of control and move toward a more fulfilling and meaningful life. The journey may be challenging, but it is possible, and you have the strength within you to make it.

Reframing Trauma as a Part of Your Life Story

Reframing trauma is a powerful tool that can help survivors regain control over their narrative and their lives. When we experience trauma, it can feel as though the event has come to define us, casting a shadow over every aspect of our existence. However, trauma is just one chapter in the story of our lives, and with the right tools and mindset, we can learn to view it as a part of our story, but not the entirety of it.

Imagine your life as a book, with each chapter representing different experiences and phases. Trauma might be a particularly intense and painful chapter, but it doesn't have to be the last one. By reframing trauma, you can start to see this chapter as a turning point, a moment of profound transformation that, while difficult, has also given you unique insights and strengths. This shift in perspective is not about minimizing the pain or the impact of the trauma, but rather about recognizing that it is one part of a larger, more complex story.

One practical way to begin the process of reframing is to explore the narrative you have constructed around your trauma. Take some time to reflect on the story you tell yourself about what happened. What are the key themes? What emotions do you associate with this story? Often, our initial narratives are filled with blame, shame, and a sense of helplessness. These narratives are understandable and valid, but they can also keep us stuck in a cycle of pain and self-doubt.

To start reframing, try to identify the parts of your story that you can challenge or reframe. For example, if you feel a deep sense of shame, ask yourself where this shame comes from. Is it something you deserve, or is it a result of the trauma itself? Recognize that trauma is something that was done to you, not something you chose or deserved. This can help you begin to separate your identity from the trauma.

Another powerful technique is to focus on the strengths and resilience you have developed as a result of your experiences. Trauma can be a crucible that forges incredible resilience, empathy, and a deeper understanding of the human condition. By acknowledging these strengths, you can start to see yourself not just as a victim of trauma, but as a survivor who has the power to shape their future.

Consider writing a new narrative for yourself, one that includes the trauma but also highlights the growth and resilience that have come from it. You might start by writing a letter to your future self, describing the person you are becoming and the goals you are working towards. This letter can serve as a reminder of your potential and a source of motivation when you face challenges.

Engage in activities that help you connect with the present moment and your values. Mindfulness practices, such as meditation or journaling, can be incredibly helpful in this process. They allow you to observe your thoughts and emotions without judgment, helping you to gain a more balanced and compassionate perspective on your experiences.

Finally, seek support from others who understand what you are going through. Joining a support group or working with a therapist can provide a safe space to share your story and receive encouragement and guidance. Sometimes, hearing others' stories of resilience and growth can inspire you to see your own journey in a new light.

Reframing trauma is a journey, and it takes time and effort. But with each step, you are reclaiming your power and rewriting your story. You are not defined by your trauma; you are defined by the courage and strength you have shown in the face of it. Embrace this journey with hope and a forward-looking mindset, and you will find that you have the capacity to create a life that is meaningful, fulfilling, and truly your own.

Chapter Two

The Core Principles of ACT

In the journey of trauma recovery, finding the right tools and strategies can make all the difference. One of the most powerful and transformative approaches available is Acceptance and Commitment Therapy, or ACT. ACT is a form of cognitive-behavioral therapy that emphasizes psychological flexibility, the ability to adapt and thrive in the face of life's challenges. At its core, ACT helps us to accept what is out of our personal control and commit to actions that enrich our lives, even in the presence of pain and difficulty.

The principles of ACT are not just theoretical; they are practical and deeply rooted in the real-life experiences of countless individuals who have found their way through the darkest moments. For those of us who have experienced trauma, these principles offer a beacon of hope and a roadmap to reclaiming our lives. By embracing the core principles of ACT, we can learn to navigate the complex emotions and memories associated with trauma, ultimately leading to a more fulfilling and meaningful existence.

One of the key principles of ACT is **acceptance**. This doesn't mean resigning ourselves to a life of suffering; rather, it means acknowledging and making room for the painful thoughts and feelings that arise from our trauma. Acceptance allows us to stop fighting against our internal experiences and instead focus on what we can control—our actions and responses. When we accept our pain, we free up mental and emotional energy that can be directed towards healing and growth.

Another crucial principle is **cognitive defusion**. This involves learning to observe our thoughts and feelings without getting entangled in them. Trauma often brings with it a flood of intrusive and distressing thoughts, but through cognitive defusion, we can gain perspective and distance. Techniques such as mindfulness and self-compassion help us to see our thoughts as just that—thoughts—rather than absolute truths. This shift in perspective can be incredibly liberating, allowing us to respond to our experiences with greater clarity and wisdom.

Being present is another foundational principle of ACT. Trauma can often pull us into the past or project us into a feared future, making it difficult to engage with the present moment. By cultivating mindfulness and presence, we can anchor ourselves in the here and now. This practice not only helps to reduce anxiety and stress but also allows us to fully experience the richness of life, even in the midst of pain.

Values play a central role in ACT. Identifying and connecting with our core values provides a compass for our actions and decisions. When we know what truly matters to us, we can make choices that align with these values, even in the face of adversity. For trauma survivors, this can be particularly empowering. By focusing on what gives our lives meaning and purpose, we can find the strength to move forward and create a life that reflects our deepest desires and aspirations.

Finally, **committed action** is the practice of taking steps that are consistent with our values, even when it's difficult. This principle is about turning our intentions into actions, no matter how small they may be. Committed action is the bridge between where we are and where we want to be. It's about making a commitment to ourselves to live a life that is rich, full, and meaningful, despite the challenges we face.

As we delve deeper into these principles, you will discover practical strategies and exercises that can help you apply them to your own life. The journey of trauma recovery is not always easy, but it is profoundly rewarding. By embracing the core principles of ACT, you can learn to coexist with your painful memories and emotions while actively pursuing a life that is meaningful and fulfilling. This chapter will provide you with the tools and insights you need to begin this transformative journey, one step at a time.

Acceptance

Acceptance is a cornerstone of Acceptance and Commitment Therapy (ACT), and it plays a crucial role in the healing process for those who have experienced trauma. When we talk about acceptance in the context of ACT, it's important to understand that it is not the same as resignation. Resignation implies giving up, surrendering to the idea that nothing can change, and accepting a fate of ongoing suffering. Acceptance, on the other hand, is about making room for difficult emotions and experiences without trying to push them away or control them. It's about acknowledging that these feelings are a part of your story, but they do not define you or limit your potential for growth and healing.

Imagine you are standing in a river, and the water is rushing past you. If you try to fight against the current, you will exhaust yourself and likely be swept away. However, if you allow the current to flow around you, you can find a way to stand more steadily and even move with the water. This is a metaphor for acceptance. When you accept your difficult emotions, you are not giving in to them; you are making space for them to be present without letting them control you. This can be a profound relief, as it frees you from the constant struggle and allows you to focus on what truly matters to you.

One of the key benefits of acceptance is that it reduces the secondary suffering that often comes from fighting against our emotions. When we resist our feelings, we create additional layers of pain and distress. For example, if you are feeling anxious about a traumatic memory, you might also feel ashamed for having these feelings, or you might worry that you will never feel better. These secondary emotions can be just as debilitating as the primary ones. By accepting your anxiety, you can let go of the shame and worry, which can significantly reduce your overall emotional burden.

Acceptance also allows you to engage more fully with the present moment. Trauma can often pull you into the past or push you into a future filled with fear and uncertainty. By accepting your current emotional state, you can ground yourself in the here and now. This presence is essential for healing, as it allows you to connect with your values and take meaningful actions that align with your goals. For instance, if you value family, acceptance can help you be more present and engaged with your loved ones, even when you are feeling distressed.

It's important to note that acceptance is not about passive acceptance of harmful situations or people. It is about accepting your internal experiences, such as your thoughts and feelings, so that you can make more effective choices about how to respond to the world around you. For example, if you are in a relationship that is causing you significant distress, accepting your feelings of pain and frustration can help you make a clear and thoughtful decision about whether to stay or leave, rather than acting out of reactivity or avoidance.

Practicing acceptance can feel challenging, especially when dealing with the intense emotions that often accompany trauma. One effective way to start is by using mindfulness techniques. Mindfulness involves observing your thoughts and feelings without judgment, as if you are a curious observer. You can try simple practices like deep breathing, where you focus on the sensation of your breath moving in and out of your body. As you breathe, allow any thoughts or emotions to arise and pass without trying to change them. This practice can help you develop a more accepting and compassionate relationship with your inner experiences.

Another helpful approach is to engage in self-compassion. When you notice yourself struggling with difficult emotions, try to offer yourself the same kindness and understanding you would offer to a friend. Speak to yourself with gentle, supportive words, and remind yourself that it's okay to feel this way. Self-compassion can be a powerful tool for acceptance, as it helps you create a safe and nurturing internal environment.

Remember, acceptance is a process, and it takes time and practice. Be patient with yourself as you learn to make room for your difficult emotions. Each step you take towards acceptance is a step towards healing and reclaiming your life. By embracing discomfort and allowing yourself to feel what you feel, you open the door to a more authentic and fulfilling life, one where your past does not dictate your future.

Cognitive Defusion

Cognitive defusion is a powerful technique in Acceptance and Commitment Therapy (ACT) that helps individuals create distance between themselves and their thoughts. When we experience trauma, our minds can become flooded with painful thoughts and beliefs that seem to define us. Cognitive defusion teaches us to see these thoughts for what they are—just words and images that pass through our minds—rather than absolute truths. This shift in perspective can be incredibly liberating, allowing us to break free from the grip of painful thoughts and beliefs.

Imagine that your thoughts are like leaves floating down a stream. Each thought is a leaf, and the stream is the flow of your mind. Instead of trying to grab and hold onto each leaf, you can simply watch them pass by. This metaphor can help you understand that your thoughts are transient and do not need to control you. For trauma survivors, this can be particularly useful in managing the recurring and often distressing thoughts that can arise.

One practical way to practice cognitive defusion is through the use of language. When a distressing thought arises, try to rephrase it in a more neutral or playful way. For example, if you find yourself thinking, "I am worthless," you might change it to, "I am having the thought that I am worthless." This simple shift in language helps you recognize that the thought is just a thought, not a fact about who you are. Another playful approach is to imagine the thought as if it were spoken by a cartoon character. This can add a layer of humor and distance, making the thought less overwhelming.

Another effective technique is to use mindfulness exercises to observe your thoughts without judgment. You can try a simple mindfulness practice where you sit in a quiet place and focus on your breath. As you breathe in and out, notice any thoughts that arise. Instead of engaging with these thoughts, simply observe them and let them pass. You might say to yourself, "There's that thought again," and then return your focus to your breath. This practice helps you develop a non-reactive stance towards your thoughts, reducing their power over you.

Visualization techniques can also be very helpful in cognitive defusion. Imagine your thoughts as clouds in the sky. Each thought is a cloud, and the sky represents your mind. Just as clouds come and go, so do your thoughts. You can watch the clouds (thoughts) drift by without getting caught up in them. This visualization can be particularly soothing and can help you maintain a sense of calm and distance from your thoughts.

For trauma survivors, cognitive defusion can be a game-changer in managing intrusive thoughts and memories. For example, if you find yourself reliving a traumatic event, you can use cognitive defusion to create some space. You might say to yourself, "I am having a memory of the traumatic event," rather than, "This is happening again." This shift in perspective can help you recognize that you are not reliving the trauma, but simply experiencing a memory. You can also use the leaf on the stream metaphor to visualize the memory as a leaf that will eventually pass.

Another practical application is to use cognitive defusion in daily activities. For instance, if you are out for a walk and a distressing thought about the trauma comes up, you can acknowledge it and then gently shift your focus to the present moment. Notice the sounds around you, the feel of the ground under your feet, and the sights you see. This practice helps ground you in the present and reduces the power of the distressing thought.

Cognitive defusion is not about ignoring or suppressing your thoughts; it's about learning to relate to them in a different way. By practicing these techniques, you can create a sense of distance and control over your thoughts, allowing you to live more fully in the present and pursue the life you want to lead. Remember, you are not your thoughts; you are the observer of your thoughts, and you have the power to choose how you respond to them.

Mindfulness

In the heart of Acceptance and Commitment Therapy (ACT) lies the practice of mindfulness, a powerful tool that can profoundly impact the journey of trauma recovery. Mindfulness is not just a technique; it is a way of being, a compassionate and non-judgmental awareness of the present moment. For those who have experienced trauma, this practice can be a lifeline, helping to anchor them in the here and now, away from the overwhelming whirlpool of past memories and future anxieties.

When we talk about mindfulness in the context of trauma recovery, we are inviting individuals to develop a new relationship with their thoughts and emotions. Trauma often leaves us feeling fragmented, as if we are constantly being pulled back to the moment of the event, or we are anxiously trying to avoid any reminders of it. Mindfulness offers a gentle yet firm anchor, helping us to stay present and grounded, even in the midst of emotional turbulence.

Imagine sitting by a river, watching the water flow by. Each leaf, each ripple, is a thought or emotion that passes through your mind. Mindfulness teaches us to observe these thoughts and emotions without getting swept away by them. Instead of struggling against the current, we learn to sit on the riverbank, observing the flow with curiosity and kindness. This perspective shift is crucial for trauma recovery because it allows us to acknowledge our pain without becoming overwhelmed by it.

One of the most transformative aspects of mindfulness is its ability to help us develop a more compassionate relationship with ourselves. Trauma can breed self-criticism and shame, making it difficult to find moments of self-compassion. Through mindfulness, we can begin to treat ourselves with the same kindness and understanding we would offer to a dear friend. When a painful memory arises, instead of pushing it away or judging ourselves for feeling it, we can simply acknowledge it, "Ah, there you are," and let it pass, knowing that it is just a part of our experience, not the whole of who we are.

Practicing mindfulness can take many forms, and finding what works best for you is a personal journey. Some find solace in traditional meditation, sitting in quiet stillness and focusing on the breath. Others may prefer more active forms of mindfulness, such as yoga or walking meditation, where the body becomes a bridge to the present moment. The key is to find a practice that resonates with you and to make it a regular part of your life.

When you sit down to meditate, or when you take a mindful walk, you are not trying to eliminate your thoughts or emotions. Instead, you are creating a space where you can observe them with clarity and without judgment. This practice can help you develop a greater sense of control over your internal experience. You begin to realize that you are not your thoughts; you are the observer of your thoughts. This realization is empowering, as it allows you to choose how you respond to your internal landscape, rather than being controlled by it.

Mindfulness also helps to cultivate a sense of safety and grounding. For many trauma survivors, the world can feel unpredictable and unsafe. Mindfulness practices can provide a sense of stability, a reminder that you are here, in this moment, and that you are safe. By focusing on the present, you can reconnect with your body and your environment, finding moments of peace and calm amidst the chaos.

In the journey of trauma recovery, mindfulness is a beacon of hope. It is a practice that can help you navigate the complex emotions and memories that come with healing. By staying present and grounded, you can find the strength and resilience to move forward, to live a life that is meaningful and fulfilling, despite the challenges you have faced. Embrace mindfulness as a supportive companion on your path, and you will discover a deeper sense of peace and self-compassion.

The Observing Self

The concept of the observing self is a cornerstone of Acceptance and Commitment Therapy (ACT) and plays a vital role in helping individuals, especially trauma survivors, to gain clarity and emotional distance from their traumatic memories. At its core, the observing self is the part of us that can step back and observe our thoughts and emotions without getting entangled in them. It's the part of us that can witness our experiences, including the most painful ones, with a sense of detachment and compassion.

For trauma survivors, the observing self can be a powerful tool in the process of healing and moving forward. When weExperience trauma, it can feel as though these experiences have taken over, making it difficult to see ourselves as separate from the pain. However, by cultivating the observing self, we can begin to see that we are not our thoughts or emotions, but rather the observer of them. This perspective can provide a crucial emotional distance, allowing us to look at our traumatic memories with a more balanced and less reactive lens.

One way to practice this is through mindfulness exercises. Mindfulness involves paying attention to the present moment with curiosity and without judgment. When you practice mindfulness, you can start to notice the thoughts and emotions that arise without immediately reacting to them. For example, you might notice a thought like, "I will never be safe again," or an emotion like fear, and instead of getting swept up in these experiences, you can acknowledge them and let them be. You might say to yourself, "I am having the thought that I will never be safe again," or "I am feeling fear right now." This simple act of labeling can create a bit of space between you and your experiences, allowing you to see them more clearly.

Another technique is to visualize the observing self as a vast, open sky, and your thoughts and emotions as clouds passing through. No matter how dark or stormy these clouds may be, they are just passing through, and the sky remains constant. This visualization can help you understand that while your thoughts and emotions are real and valid, they are not all of who you are. You are the sky, the constant, unchanging part that can witness and hold all of your experiences.

For trauma survivors, this perspective can be transformative. It can help you see that while your traumatic memories are a part of your story, they do not define you. You are more than your trauma, and you have the capacity to observe and hold these experiences with compassion and understanding. This can be a stepping stone to recognizing the strengths and resilience you have developed through your journey.

By practicing the observing self, you can begin to see your thoughts and emotions as transient and understandable reactions to your experiences, rather than fixed aspects of your identity. This can help you gain a sense of control and agency, allowing you to navigate your emotions and thoughts with more ease and less reactivity. It's about creating a space where you can acknowledge your pain without being consumed by it, and from there, you can start to make choices that align with your values and the life you want toLive.

This process is not about erasing your pain or pretending it doesn't exist. It's about finding a way to coexist with your painful memories and emotions while still moving forward in a direction that matters to you. By fostering the observing self, you can cultivate a more compassionate and balanced relationship with yourself, paving the way for a life that is meaningful and fulfilling, despite the challenges you have faced.

Values

In the world of Acceptance and Commitment Therapy (ACT), values play a central role in guiding individuals towards a more fulfilling and meaningful life. This is especially true for those who have experienced trauma, as the process of reconnecting with one's values can provide a sense of direction and purpose, even in the face of overwhelming pain and adversity.

Values are the things that matter most to you—your inner compass, if you will. They are the principles and qualities that you hold dear and that give your life meaning. When we experience trauma, it can feel as though these values have been shattered or lost. The world might seem dark and devoid of the things that once brought us joy and purpose. However, the beauty of ACT lies in its ability to help us rediscover and recommit to these values, even after the most challenging experiences.

Understanding your values is the first step in this journey. It involves taking a deep, honest look at what truly matters to you. What are the things that, when you think about them, bring a sense of warmth and significance to your heart? Maybe it's your relationships with family and friends, your commitment to personal growth, your passion for helping others, or your desire to live a life of integrity and authenticity. Whatever your values are, they are unique to you, and they are the foundation upon which you can rebuild your life.

Reconnecting with your values is not just about remembering them; it's about actively living them. This means making choices and taking actions that align with what you hold dear. For example, if one of your core values is compassion, you might start by reaching out to a friend who is going through a tough time or volunteering at a local charity. If your value is personal growth, you might commit to learning a new skill or pursuing a long-abandoned hobby. These actions, no matter how small, can help you feel more connected to yourself and the world around you.

One of the most powerful aspects of values in ACT is that they provide a sense of direction and purpose. When you are clear about what you value, you have a roadmap for your life. This can be incredibly empowering, especially after trauma, when it's easy to feel lost and directionless. By focusing on your values, you can set goals and make decisions that are in line with who you are and what you want to achieve. This can help you move forward with confidence and resilience, even when the path ahead is uncertain.

Moreover, values can serve as a source of strength and motivation. When the going gets tough, and it will, having a clear sense of what matters most to you can be a powerful anchor. It can help you stay grounded and focused, reminding you why you are doing what you are doing. This is particularly important in trauma recovery, where the road can be long and filled with setbacks. Knowing that your actions are aligned with your values can give you the courage to keep going, even when the pain feels overwhelming.

It's also important to recognize that values are not static; they can evolve over time. As you grow and change, your values may shift, and that's okay. The process of reconnecting with your values is an ongoing one, and it's about being open to what you discover about yourself along the way. This openness and flexibility are key components of ACT, as they allow you to adapt and grow, even in the face of adversity.

In the context of trauma recovery, values can be a lifeline. They can help you rebuild a sense of self and identity that has been shattered by the trauma. By living your values, you are not just surviving; you are thriving. You are creating a life that is meaningful and fulfilling, a life that reflects who you are and what you stand for. This is the essence of trauma-focused ACT—using the principles of ACT to help you not just manage your pain, but to live a life that is rich, full, and true to yourself.

So, as you begin this journey of reconnecting with your values, remember that you are not alone. Reach out to others who can support you, whether it's friends, family, or a therapist. Share your values with them, and let them be a part of your journey. Together, you can create a future that is filled with hope, purpose, and the things that truly matter to you.

Committed Action

Committed action is a cornerstone of Acceptance and Commitment Therapy (ACT) and plays a crucial role in helping trauma survivors take small, meaningful steps toward recovery and living a life aligned with their values. When we talk about committed action, we're not just referring to grand gestures or monumental changes. Instead, it's about the consistent, deliberate efforts you make each day to move in the direction of your values, even when it feels challenging or uncomfortable.

Imagine you're on a long journey, and the path ahead is rugged and sometimes obscured by fog. This journey represents your recovery process. Committed action is like taking one step at a time, even when the terrain is difficult. Each step might seem small, but collectively, they lead you closer to your destination. The key is persistence. Healing from trauma is not a sprint; it's a marathon. It requires a steady, unwavering commitment to your values and the life you want to live.

One of the unique aspects of committed action in trauma-focused ACT is the emphasis on values. Values are the guiding principles that give your life direction and meaning. They are the "why" behind your actions. For trauma survivors, reconnecting with these values can be a powerful motivator. Perhaps your values include relationships, personal growth, creativity, or making a positive impact in the world. By identifying and committing to these values, you can start to build a life that feels purposeful and fulfilling, even in the face of past trauma.

Let's consider an example. Suppose you value helping others. This value might have been overshadowed by the trauma you've experienced, making it hard to imagine how you can contribute to the world. Committed action in this context could start with small steps, such as volunteering for a few hours at a local charity, reaching out to a friend who needs support, or even writing a letter to someone who has inspired you. Each of these actions aligns with your value of helping others and can gradually build your confidence and sense of purpose.

Another important aspect of committed action is the willingness to face discomfort. Trauma can create a lot of emotional and psychological pain, and the natural instinct is often to avoid these feelings. However, avoiding discomfort can keep you stuck. Committed action involves acknowledging the discomfort and choosing to move forward anyway. This doesn't mean you have to jump into the deep end immediately; it means taking small, manageable steps that challenge you to grow.

For instance, if you value personal growth and have been avoiding certain activities because they trigger painful memories, you might start by reading a book on resilience or attending a support group meeting. These actions might be uncomfortable at first, but they are steps toward living a life that aligns with your values. Over time, as you take more steps, you'll build a sense of mastery and control over your life.

Persistence is another key element of committed action. Healing from trauma is not a linear process. There will be setbacks and times when you feel like giving up. It's important to remember that these moments are part of the journey. When you encounter obstacles, take a moment to reflect on your values and the reasons why you are committed to this path. Remind yourself that each small step you take, no matter how insignificant it may seem, is a step toward a better future.

To stay motivated, it can be helpful to celebrate your progress, no matter how small. Keep a journal of the steps you take and the progress you make. Reflect on how far you've come and the challenges you've overcome. This can provide a sense of accomplishment and reinforce your commitment to your values.

In the end, committed action is about more than just taking steps; it's about the mindset you bring to those steps. It's about approaching each day with a sense of purpose and a willingness to face the challenges that come your way. By focusing on your values and taking consistent, meaningful actions, you can gradually build a life that is rich, full, and meaningful. Healing is a journey, and with each step you take, you are reclaiming your life and moving toward the future you envision.

Chapter 3

Acceptance – Letting Go of the Struggle Against Pain

"Acceptance is not about giving up, but about finding the strength to move forward, even when the path is difficult."

When we talk about acceptance in the context of trauma, it's natural to feel a sense of resistance. The idea of accepting pain and emotional turmoil might seem counterintuitive, especially when our instinct is to fight against it, to push it away, and to seek relief. However, the journey of healing from trauma is not about erasing the past or pretending that the pain doesn't exist. It's about finding a way to live with the pain, to integrate it into your life story, and to move forward with a renewed sense of purpose and resilience.

Imagine a river that flows through a rocky landscape. The river doesn't try to remove the rocks; instead, it finds a way to flow around them, to adapt and continue its journey. In the same way, acceptance is about finding the strength to flow around the obstacles of trauma, rather than getting stuck in the struggle against them. This chapter is about helping you understand and embrace the concept of acceptance as a powerful tool for healing and moving forward.

Acceptance is not about giving up or resigning yourself to a life of pain. It's about acknowledging the reality of your experiences and the emotions they have brought, without judgment. It's about recognizing that pain is a part of your journey, but it does not define who you are or what you can become. By accepting your pain, you are not condoning it or saying it was okay. Instead, you are making a conscious choice to stop fighting a battle that you cannot win, and to redirect your energy towards growth and healing.

Think of it this way: when you're in the midst of a storm, you can't control the wind or the rain, but you can control how you respond to it. You can choose to fight against the storm, which might leave you exhausted and more vulnerable, or you can find a way to shelter yourself and wait for the storm to pass. Acceptance is like finding that shelter. It's a place of safety where you can gather your strength, reflect on your experiences, and prepare for the next steps in your journey.

This chapter will guide you through the process of acceptance, offering practical strategies and compassionate insights to help you let go of the struggle against pain. We will explore how acceptance can lead to greater psychological flexibility, allowing you to navigate your emotions with more ease and to engage more fully in the life you want to live. We will also delve into the role of mindfulness and self-compassion in the acceptance process, providing you with tools to cultivate a more positive and hopeful outlook.

Remember, the goal of acceptance is not to make the pain disappear but to find a way to live with it that is sustainable and fulfilling. It's about recognizing that you are more than your trauma, that you have the capacity to heal, and that you have the strength to move forward, even in the face of adversity. As you read through this chapter, allow yourself to be open to the idea of acceptance, and trust that it can be a transformative part of your healing journey.

What Does It Mean to Accept Trauma?

Acceptance is a profound and often misunderstood concept, especially in the context of trauma. It is not about resignation or giving up; rather, it is about recognizing and allowing the pain to exist without letting it define or control you. When we talk about accepting trauma, we are talking about a process that involves deep self-compassion and a willingness to face the difficult emotions that come with it.

Imagine for a moment that you are holding a heavy stone in your hand. This stone represents your trauma. You might try to throw it away, but it keeps coming back. You might try to hide it, but it still weighs you down.

Acceptance is like gently placing the stone on the ground and standing next to it. You acknowledge its presence, but you no longer carry it with you everywhere you go. You recognize that the stone is a part of your life, but it does not have to dictate your every move.

Acceptance begins with acknowledging the reality of your pain. It means saying, "Yes, this happened to me, and it was incredibly painful." This acknowledgment is not an admission of defeat; it is a courageous act of recognizing the truth of your experience. By accepting the reality of your trauma, you are taking the first step towards healing. You are saying, "I see you, pain, and I understand that you are a part of my story."

However, acceptance goes beyond mere acknowledgment. It involves a shift in how you relate to your pain. Instead of fighting against it or trying to suppress it, you allow yourself to feel the emotions that come with it. This might seem counterintuitive, especially if you have spent years trying to avoid or numb these feelings. But the truth is, when we try to push our pain away, it often becomes more persistent and overwhelming.

Think of it like a wave in the ocean. When you try to fight against the wave, it can knock you down and drag you under. But if you learn to swim with the wave, to let it move through you, you can emerge on the other side with a sense of balance and control. Acceptance is like learning to swim with the waves of your emotions. You allow them to come and go, knowing that they are temporary and that you have the strength to navigate them.

One of the most important aspects of acceptance is self-compassion. It is about treating yourself with the same kindness and understanding that you would offer to a friend. When you are in pain, it is natural to feel a range of emotions, from anger and sadness to fear and confusion. Instead of judging these feelings as "wrong" or "bad," you can practice self-compassion by acknowledging them and offering yourself gentle support.

For example, you might say to yourself, "It's okay to feel sad. This is a natural response to what I've been through." By validating your emotions, you create a safe space within yourself where you can process and heal. Self-compassion also involves recognizing that you are doing the best you can, even if it feels like you are struggling. You are not alone in your pain, and it is okay to seek help and support from others.

Another key aspect of acceptance is understanding that your trauma does not define you. While it is a significant part of your life story, it is not the whole story. You are a multifaceted individual with strengths, talents, and a unique perspective on the world. Acceptance allows you to see yourself in a more holistic and compassionate light. You can acknowledge the impact of your trauma while also recognizing the resilience and growth that have come from it.

Practicing acceptance is a process, and it takes time and patience. It is not something you do once and then move on; it is a continuous journey of self-discovery and healing. You might find it helpful to engage in mindfulness practices, such as meditation or deep breathing, to help you stay present and connected to your emotions. These practices can provide a sense of grounding and help you cultivate a more accepting attitude towards your experiences.

Remember, acceptance is not about forgetting or ignoring your pain. It is about making peace with the past so that you can live more fully in the present. By accepting your trauma, you are taking a powerful step towards reclaiming your life and pursuing the meaningful, fulfilling future you deserve. You are not defined by your pain; you are defined by your courage and your capacity to grow and heal. Embrace this journey with an open heart and a nurturing spirit, and you will find that you have the strength to navigate even the most challenging of waters.

Why We Resist Acceptance

Acceptance is a cornerstone of Trauma-Focused Acceptance and Commitment Therapy (TF-ACT), yet it is often one of the most challenging aspects for survivors to embrace. The very idea of accepting trauma can feel counterintuitive, even impossible, for those who have experienced profound pain and suffering. Understanding why trauma survivors resist acceptance can provide a compassionate lens through which to view this struggle and offer a pathway toward healing.

One of the primary reasons trauma survivors resist acceptance is fear. Fear is a natural and instinctive response to trauma, a mechanism that evolved to protect us from danger. However, when the danger has passed, this fear can persist, manifesting as anxiety, hypervigilance, and a constant state of alertness. The thought of accepting the trauma can trigger a wave of fear, as if acknowledging the event might somehow make it real or make it happen again. This fear can be paralyzing, leading survivors to avoid any thoughts or feelings related to the trauma, a behavior known as emotional avoidance.

Denial is another common barrier to acceptance. Denial is a powerful defense mechanism that helps us cope with overwhelming emotions by blocking out the reality of the trauma. It can provide a temporary sense of relief, allowing survivors to function in their daily lives. However, denial can also prevent healing, as it keeps the trauma locked away, unprocessed and unresolved. The act of denial can be subtle, manifesting as a refusal to talk about the trauma, a belief that it didn't happen, or a insistence that it's not as bad as it seems. Over time, this denial can create a rift between the survivor's inner world and their external reality, leading to feelings of disconnection and isolation.

Shame is another profound barrier to acceptance. Trauma often leaves survivors feeling deeply ashamed, as if the event was somehow their fault or a reflection of their worth. This shame can be internalized, leading to a harsh inner critic that constantly berates the survivor for not being strong enough, smart enough, or good enough to prevent the trauma. The idea of accepting the trauma can feel like a confirmation of these negative beliefs, making it incredibly difficult to let go of the struggle against pain. Shame can also manifest as a fear of judgment from others, leading survivors to hide their pain and struggle alone.

Understanding these psychological and emotional barriers can help us approach the journey of acceptance with greater compassion and patience. It's important to recognize that resistance to acceptance is not a sign of weakness or a lack of willpower, but a natural response to an overwhelming and life-altering event. The process of acceptance is not about forgetting the trauma or condoning what happened, but about finding a way to live with the pain without being controlled by it.

If you find yourself struggling with acceptance, know that you are not alone. It's okay to feel afraid, to deny the reality of what happened, and to experience deep shame. These feelings are valid and understandable. The key is to approach them with curiosity and kindness, rather than judgment. When you notice these feelings arising, try to observe them without reacting. Ask yourself, "What is this fear trying to protect me from? What is this denial helping me avoid? What is this shame telling me about myself?"

By gently exploring these questions, you can begin to unravel the layers of resistance and create space for acceptance. Remember, acceptance is not a one-time event but a ongoing process. It's about making a commitment to face your pain, to understand it, and to find a way to live with it that aligns with your values and goals. With time, patience, and support, you can learn to let go of the struggle against pain and find a path toward healing and a more fulfilling life.

Exercises for Practicing Acceptance

Cultivating acceptance is a crucial step in the journey of healing from trauma. It involves letting go of the struggle against pain and learning to coexist with difficult emotions and thoughts. This doesn't mean you have to like or enjoy these feelings, but rather that you acknowledge their presence and allow them to be part of your experience without fighting against them. Here are several practical exercises that can help you cultivate acceptance in your daily life:

One powerful way to begin is through mindfulness meditation. Find a quiet and comfortable place where you can sit or lie down without distractions. Close your eyes and take a few deep breaths to center yourself. As you breathe, bring your attention to the sensations in your body. Notice any areas of tension or discomfort, and simply observe them without trying to change them. If your mind starts to wander, gently guide it back to your breath. This practice helps you develop a non-judgmental awareness of your present moment, allowing you to accept what is without resistance.

Journaling is another excellent tool for cultivating acceptance. Set aside a few minutes each day to write down your thoughts and feelings. Start by describing what you are experiencing, whether it's a painful memory, a difficult emotion, or a physical sensation. As you write, try to describe these experiences with curiosity and compassion. Ask yourself, "What is this feeling trying to tell me?" or "How can I be kind to myself in this moment?" Writing can help you process your experiences and gain a deeper understanding of your inner world, making it easier to accept what you are feeling.

Body-awareness practices can also be incredibly helpful. Try a body scan meditation, where you systematically bring your attention to different parts of your body, starting from your toes and moving up to the top of your head. Notice any sensations, whether they are pleasant, unpleasant, or neutral. If you find areas of tension or discomfort, imagine breathing warmth and relaxation into those areas. This practice helps you connect with your body and accept it as it is, rather than trying to force it to feel a certain way.

Another useful exercise is the "Leaves on a Stream" visualization. Imagine you are sitting by a gently flowing stream, and each thought or feeling that arises is like a leaf floating on the water. As you observe these leaves, you don't try to grab them or push them away; you simply watch them as they float by. This visualization helps you develop a sense of detachment from your thoughts and feelings, allowing you to see them as transient and not defining parts of who you are.

Engaging in self-compassion practices can also foster acceptance. When you notice yourself struggling with difficult emotions, try offering yourself words of kindness and understanding. You might say something like, "It's okay to feel this way. I am here for you, and I accept you just as you are." This practice can help you develop a more compassionate and accepting relationship with yourself.

Finally, consider incorporating gratitude into your daily routine. Each day, take a moment to reflect on three things you are grateful for, no matter how small they may seem. This practice can help shift your focus from what is painful to what is positive in your life, fostering a sense of acceptance and contentment.

By incorporating these practices into your daily life, you can gradually build your capacity for acceptance. Remember, the goal is not to eliminate pain but to learn how to live with it in a way that allows you to pursue a meaningful and fulfilling life. Each step you take in this journey is a step towards reclaiming your power and regaining control over your narrative.

Accepting Emotions without Judgment

Accepting emotions without attaching judgment to them is a cornerstone of trauma recovery and a fundamental principle of Trauma-Focused Acceptance and Commitment Therapy (TF-ACT). When we experience trauma, our emotions can feel overwhelming and uncontrollable, often leading us to judge ourselves harshly for feeling the way we do. This judgment can create a secondary layer of suffering, making it even harder to heal and move forward. By learning to accept our emotions as they are, without judgment, we can begin to break this cycle and find a path to greater psychological flexibility and resilience.

Imagine for a moment that you are standing on the shore of a vast, turbulent ocean. The waves represent your emotions—sometimes calm, sometimes violent. When you judge your emotions, it's like trying to fight against the waves, struggling to keep your head above water. This struggle can be exhausting and often leaves you feeling more overwhelmed and helpless. On the other hand, when you accept your emotions, it's like learning to swim with the waves, allowing them to move through you without being swept away by them.

Accepting emotions without judgment is not about denying or suppressing them; it's about acknowledging them for what they are and understanding that they are a natural part of the human experience. When you feel a surge of anger, sadness, or fear, try to observe it without labeling it as good or bad. Instead, say to yourself, "I am feeling angry right now," or "I am feeling sad." This simple act of naming your emotion can help you create a bit of distance from it, making it easier to manage.

One powerful way to practice this is through mindfulness. Mindfulness involves being present in the moment and observing your thoughts and feelings without judgment. You can start by setting aside a few minutes each day to sit quietly and focus on your breath. As you breathe, notice any emotions that arise. When you feel a strong emotion, gently acknowledge it and let it be. You might say to yourself, "I notice that I am feeling anxious," and then return your focus to your breath. Over time, this practice can help you develop a more compassionate and accepting relationship with your emotions.

Judgment often leads to more suffering because it creates a cycle of negative self-talk and self-criticism. When you judge yourself for feeling a certain way, you add a layer of guilt and shame to the already painful experience. For example, if you feel anxious and tell yourself, "I shouldn't feel this way," you are likely to feel even more anxious and inadequate. This self-criticism can spiral into a deeper sense of helplessness and despair.

Instead, try to approach your emotions with curiosity and kindness. Ask yourself, "What is this emotion trying to tell me?" and "What do I need right now to take care of myself?" By treating yourself with the same compassion you would offer a close friend, you can begin to heal and find a sense of peace.

For instance, if you are feeling overwhelmed by a wave of grief, you might take a moment to pause and acknowledge the depth of your pain. You could say to yourself, "It's okay to feel this way. Grief is a natural response to loss." Then, you might engage in a self-care activity that brings you comfort, such as listening to a soothing piece of music, writing in a journal, or reaching out to a supportive friend.

Remember, accepting emotions without judgment is not about passively giving in to them; it's about recognizing that they are a part of your experience and that you have the strength to navigate them. By practicing acceptance, you can break free from the cycle of judgment and suffering, and begin to reclaim your life. This practice is a powerful tool in your journey of trauma recovery, helping you to find a sense of control and peace, even in the face of difficult emotions.

Long-Term Benefits of Acceptance in Trauma Healing

Practicing acceptance is a transformative journey that can bring about profound and lasting changes in your psychological and emotional well-being. When you learn to accept your painful thoughts and experiences, you are not condoning them or resigning yourself to a life of suffering. Instead, you are making a conscious choice to let go of the struggle against pain, which can lead to greater emotional resilience, self-awareness, and a sense of inner peace.

One of the most significant long-term benefits of practicing acceptance is the development of emotional resilience. When you accept your emotions, you no longer fight against them or try to push them away. This shift in mindset allows you to experience your feelings fully, without judgment. Over time, this practice helps you build a stronger emotional foundation. You become more adept at handling a wide range of emotions, both positive and negative, without being overwhelmed by them. This resilience is crucial in the face of future challenges, as it enables you to bounce back more quickly and maintain a sense of stability.

Acceptance also fosters a deeper sense of self-awareness. By allowing yourself to acknowledge and accept your thoughts and feelings, you gain a clearer understanding of your inner world. This self-awareness is not just about recognizing what you are feeling; it's about understanding the underlying causes and patterns that drive those feelings. For instance, you might realize that certain triggers consistently bring up feelings of anxiety or sadness. With this knowledge, you can develop more effective strategies for managing these triggers, rather than reacting impulsively or avoiding them altogether. This heightened self-awareness is a powerful tool for personal growth and can lead to more authentic and fulfilling relationships with others.

Another key benefit of acceptance is the sense of peace it brings. When you stop fighting against your pain, you create space for a more peaceful and balanced state of mind. This doesn't mean that the pain disappears entirely; rather, it means that you no longer add to your suffering by resisting what is. Acceptance allows you to be present with your emotions, to sit with them, and to let them pass naturally. This can be a profound relief, as it breaks the cycle of constant struggle and allows you to find moments of calm and clarity even in the midst of difficulty.

Moreover, practicing acceptance can lead to a more optimistic and forward-looking outlook on life. When you are no longer consumed by the struggle against pain, you have more mental and emotional energy to focus on what truly matters to you. You can set meaningful goals, pursue your passions, and build a life that aligns with your values. This shift in focus can be incredibly empowering, as it allows you to take control of your narrative and actively shape your future. Instead of being defined by your past traumas, you can choose to define yourself by your resilience, your growth, and your capacity for joy and fulfillment.

It's important to remember that the journey of acceptance is not always easy, and it requires commitment and practice. There will be times when the struggle feels overwhelming, and it might be tempting to revert to old patterns of resistance. But with each step you take towards acceptance, you are building a stronger, more resilient self. You are learning to navigate the complexities of your emotions with grace and compassion. And as you do, you will find that you are not just surviving; you are thriving.

So, as you continue on this path, be gentle with yourself. Celebrate the small victories and be patient with the challenges. Each moment of acceptance is a step towards a more peaceful, resilient, and fulfilling life. Stay committed to this practice, and you will discover the profound benefits it can bring to every aspect of your being.

Chapter 4

Separating Yourself from Traumatic Thoughts

"Between stimulus and response, there is a space. In that space is our power to choose our response. In our response lies our growth and our freedom."
Viktor E. Frankl

In the journey of trauma recovery, one of the most powerful tools you can wield is the ability to create space between yourself and your traumatic thoughts. This chapter delves into the concept of cognitive defusion, a cornerstone of Trauma-Focused Acceptance and Commitment Therapy (TF-ACT), and explores how it can help you regain control over your life.

Imagine for a moment that your mind is like a vast library, filled with countless books. Each book represents a thought, a memory, or an emotion. For many of us, the books that hold our traumatic experiences are often the ones we find ourselves revisiting, their pages dog-eared and worn from frequent handling. These thoughts can feel so real, so immediate, that they seem to define who we are and what we are capable of. But what if I told you that you don't have to be bound by these books? What if you could learn to read them without being consumed by their content?

Cognitive defusion is the process of stepping back from your thoughts and seeing them for what they are— just thoughts, not facts. It's about recognizing that the stories in your mind, no matter how vivid or distressing, do not have to control your actions or your life. By practicing cognitive defusion, you can create that crucial space between the stimulus of a traumatic memory and your response to it. This space is where your power to choose lies.

Let's consider a common scenario: a person who has experienced a traumatic event might often think, "I am broken and will never be whole again." This thought can feel so intense and true that it can paralyze them, preventing them from moving forward. But with cognitive defusion, they can learn to say, "I am having the thought that I am broken and will never be whole again." This subtle shift in language helps to separate the person from the thought, making it easier to challenge and eventually let go of it.

Cognitive defusion is not about denying the reality of what you have experienced or the emotions that come with it. Instead, it's about acknowledging the presence of these thoughts without letting them dictate your life. It's about learning to observe your thoughts with curiosity and compassion, rather than judgment and fear. By doing so, you can begin to see that your thoughts are just one part of who you are, not the whole story.

In this chapter, we will explore various techniques and exercises that can help you practice cognitive defusion. We will delve into how mindfulness, language, and imagery can be powerful tools in creating that essential space between you and your thoughts. We will also discuss how to integrate cognitive defusion into your daily life, making it a natural part of your trauma recovery journey.

Remember, the goal is not to eliminate painful thoughts and memories but to learn how to live with them in a way that allows you to pursue a meaningful and fulfilling life. As you read on, I encourage you to approach this chapter with an open mind and a willingness to explore new ways of thinking. With each step you take, you are reclaiming your power and moving closer to the life you want to live.

Understanding Cognitive Defusion

Cognitive defusion is a powerful technique within the framework of Trauma-Focused Acceptance and Commitment Therapy (TF-ACT) that helps individuals separate themselves from their thoughts, particularly those that are traumatic and distressing. At its core, cognitive defusion is about recognizing that thoughts are just thoughts—mental events that come and go, rather than absolute truths about reality. This understanding can be transformative for trauma survivors who often find themselves overwhelmed by intrusive and painful thoughts that seem to define their reality.

Imagine, for a moment, that your thoughts are like leaves floating down a stream. Each leaf represents a thought, and the stream is the continuous flow of your mind. When you practice cognitive defusion, you learn to observe these leaves without trying to grab onto them or push them away. Instead, you simply watch them as they drift by, recognizing that they are transient and not a fixed part of you. This perspective can be incredibly liberating, as it allows you to step back from the intensity of your thoughts and see them for what they are—just mental events.

For trauma survivors, this skill is particularly crucial. Traumatic memories and the thoughts that accompany them can be so vivid and intense that they feel like they are happening all over again. Cognitive defusion helps break this cycle by teaching you to recognize the difference between the thought and the event itself. When you can see that a traumatic memory is just a thought, it loses some of its power to cause emotional distress. This doesn't mean that the memory or the associated emotions disappear entirely, but it does mean that you can manage them more effectively.

One of the key benefits of cognitive defusion is that it reduces the emotional impact of traumatic thoughts. When you are no longer fused with your thoughts, you can approach them with curiosity and compassion rather than fear and avoidance. For example, if a traumatic memory arises, you might say to yourself, "I'm having the thought that I'm in danger," rather than, "I am in danger." This subtle shift in language can make a significant difference in how you experience the thought. By labeling it as a thought, you create a bit of distance, which can help you stay grounded in the present moment.

Cognitive defusion also helps you develop a more flexible and adaptive way of thinking. Instead of getting stuck in rigid patterns of thought, you can explore different perspectives and consider a broader range of possibilities. This flexibility is essential for trauma survivors, who often struggle with feelings of helplessness and a narrow focus on danger or threat. By practicing defusion, you can expand your mental horizons and open up to new experiences and opportunities.

In the context of TF-ACT, cognitive defusion is not just a technique but a way of relating to your internal world. It's about cultivating a mindful and compassionate attitude toward your thoughts, even the most difficult ones. This approach can be incredibly empowering, as it gives you a sense of control over your mental landscape. You learn that you don't have to be a passive recipient of your thoughts; you can choose how to respond to them.

As you practice cognitive defusion, you may find that the emotional intensity of your traumatic thoughts begins to diminish. This doesn't mean that you will never experience distressing thoughts again, but it does mean that you will have the tools to manage them more effectively. Over time, you can develop a greater sense of psychological flexibility, which is the ability to be present, open, and engaged, even in the face of challenging thoughts and emotions.

In essence, cognitive defusion is a powerful tool for trauma survivors because it helps you regain a sense of agency and control over your life. By learning to separate yourself from your thoughts, you can move forward with greater clarity and purpose, even as you carry the weight of your past. This skill is a cornerstone of TF-ACT, and it can be a vital step in your journey toward healing and a more fulfilling life.

The Problem with Over-Identifying with Thoughts

In the journey of healing from trauma, one of the most profound challenges we face is the way our thoughts can entangle us, deepening our emotional pain and perpetuating trauma symptoms. It's a common experience to find ourselves caught in a relentless loop of negative thoughts, each one reinforcing the last, creating a dense web of suffering that can feel inescapable. When we over-identify with these thoughts, they become more than just passing mental events; they become defining aspects of our identity. "I am broken," "I will never be safe," "The world is a dangerous place"—these are not just thoughts; they become the narrative of our lives, shaping how we see ourselves and the world around us.

This over-identification is a powerful force. It can make us feel as though our traumatic experiences are not just part of our past but are ongoing, present realities. The more we believe these thoughts, the more they influence our emotions, behaviors, and even our physical well-being. This cycle is self-perpetuating: the more we believe our thoughts, the more we feel the pain, and the more pain we feel, the more we believe our thoughts. It's a vicious cycle that can seem impossible to break.

Cognitive defusion, a core principle of Trauma-Focused Acceptance and Commitment Therapy (TF-ACT), offers a powerful tool to break this cycle. Defusion is about creating space between you and your thoughts. It's about recognizing that thoughts are just mental events, not absolute truths. When you defuse from your thoughts, you learn to observe them without getting caught up in their content. You begin to see them for what they are—words and images that come and go, like clouds in the sky.

Imagine a thought like a leaf floating down a stream. You can watch it as it passes by, without trying to grab it or push it away. You don't have to believe it or act on it; you just let it be. This perspective can be incredibly liberating. It allows you to step back from the narrative of your trauma and see it from a different angle. Instead of being overwhelmed by the thought, "I am broken," you might recognize it as just a thought, a product of your mind trying to make sense of a difficult experience. This recognition doesn't mean you ignore your pain or deny your experiences; it means you no longer let those thoughts define you.

Through cognitive defusion, you can begin to separate yourself from the painful thoughts and memories that have been holding you back. You can learn to observe them with curiosity and compassion, rather than fear and judgment. This process is not about erasing your thoughts or pretending they don't exist; it's about changing your relationship with them. When you can see your thoughts as just thoughts, you gain a sense of control and agency.

You can choose how to respond to them, rather than being controlled by them.

In the context of trauma, this shift can be transformative. It can help you break free from the patterns of thinking that have kept you stuck in the past and open up new possibilities for the present and future. By practicing cognitive defusion, you can regain a sense of psychological flexibility, allowing you to move forward with a greater sense of resilience and purpose. You can learn to coexist with your traumatic thoughts and memories, without letting them dictate your life. This is a powerful step towards regaining control and living a life that is meaningful and fulfilling, despite the challenges you have faced.

Defusion Techniques for Traumatic Memories

Cognitive defusion techniques help you separate yourself from your thoughts, reducing their emotional power and allowing you to regain a sense of control. Two particularly effective techniques are "Name the Story" and "Leaves on a Stream." Let's explore how you can use these techniques to manage the intense and often overwhelming thoughts that can arise from traumatic experiences.

First, let's dive into "Name the Story." This technique involves recognizing and labeling the recurring narratives that your mind tends to play over and over again. Traumatic experiences often create deeply ingrained stories that can feel like they define you. For example, you might find yourself thinking, "I'm not safe," or "I'm damaged beyond repair." By naming these stories, you can begin to see them as just that—stories. You can say to yourself, "This is the 'I'm not safe' story," or "This is the 'I'm damaged' story." When you name the story, you create a small but crucial distance between yourself and the thought. This distance allows you to observe the story without being fully consumed by it. You might notice that the story is just a collection of words and images, not an absolute truth about who you are or what you can become. By practicing this technique, you can start to see that you are more than your thoughts and that these stories do not have to dictate your life.

Now, let's move on to "Leaves on a Stream." This technique is a mindfulness exercise that helps you visualize your thoughts as leaves floating down a stream. Find a quiet and comfortable place to sit or lie down. Close your eyes and imagine a gentle stream flowing in front of you. As you breathe in and out, allow each thought that comes into your mind to be represented by a leaf. Watch as each leaf floats down the stream, carrying your thoughts away. You might think, "I'm not safe," and see a leaf with that thought written on it. Allow the leaf to float away, and as it does, notice that the thought begins to lose its grip on you. You can continue to breathe and watch as more leaves carrying different thoughts float by. Some leaves might carry positive thoughts, while others might carry negative ones. The key is to observe each thought without judgment, allowing it to pass by without getting caught up in it. This practice helps you develop a non-reactive awareness of your thoughts, reducing their emotional impact and helping you stay grounded in the present moment.

Both "Name the Story" and "Leaves on a Stream" are powerful techniques that can be practiced regularly to build your cognitive defusion skills. As you become more proficient, you'll find that you can more easily recognize and detach from the thoughts that stem from your traumatic experiences. This detachment is not about ignoring or suppressing your thoughts; it's about seeing them for what they are—just thoughts—and not allowing them to control your actions or emotions. By practicing these techniques, you can create a space between yourself and your thoughts, a space where you can make choices that align with your values and goals, rather than being driven by the pain of the past.

Shifting Perspective: Viewing Thoughts as Temporary

Healing from trauma, one of the most powerful tools at our disposal is the ability to see our thoughts for what they truly are: temporary, fleeting events in the mind, rather than immutable facts. This concept, known as cognitive defusion, is a cornerstone of Trauma-Focused Acceptance and Commitment Therapy (TF-ACT). It invites us to step back from the grip of our thoughts and observe them with a sense of curiosity and distance, rather than becoming entangled in their web.

Trauma has a unique way of distorting our perception of reality. When we experience a traumatic event, the intense emotions and overwhelming sensations can create a deep-seated belief that our thoughts are not just thoughts, but absolute truths. This illusion of permanence can be incredibly debilitating. We might find ourselves thinking, "I will never be the same again," or "This pain will always be with me." These thoughts can feel as solid and unmovable as the ground beneath our feet, but the truth is, they are not.

When we practice cognitive defusion, we learn to recognize that these thoughts are just mental events, passing through our minds like clouds in the sky. They come and go, and while they may be intense and powerful, they do not have the final say over our lives. By cultivating this perspective, we can begin to break free from the chains of trauma and regain a sense of control and flexibility.

Imagine for a moment that you are standing on a riverbank, watching the water flow by. Each thought is like a leaf floating on the surface of the river. Some leaves are small and insignificant, while others are large and seem to command our attention. But no matter how big or small, they are all just leaves, carried by the current and eventually passing out of sight. When we see our thoughts in this way, we can let them come and go without getting swept away by them.

This shift in perspective is not about denying the reality of our experiences or the pain they have caused. It is about recognizing that our thoughts are not the same as the events themselves. Trauma can make us feel stuck, as if we are reliving the same painful moments over and over again. But when we practice cognitive defusion, we can start to see that these thoughts are just echoes of the past, not the present reality. We can choose to acknowledge them, feel the emotions they bring, and then gently let them go.

By adopting this more flexible mindset, we open the door to a world of possibilities. We can begin to explore new ways of thinking and behaving that align with our values and goals. Instead of being held back by the weight of our thoughts, we can move forward with a sense of purpose and direction. This is the essence of trauma-focused ACT: to help us coexist with our painful memories and emotions while actively pursuing a meaningful, fulfilling life.

So, the next time you find yourself caught in a spiral of traumatic thoughts, take a deep breath and remind yourself that these thoughts are just passing mental events. They do not define you, and they do not have to control you. With practice and patience, you can learn to see them for what they are and choose a path that leads to greater freedom and well-being.

The Long-Term Impact of Cognitive Defusion on Trauma Recovery

As you delve deeper into the practice of cognitive defusion, you may begin to notice a profound transformation in how you relate to your traumatic thoughts and experiences. This shift is not just a fleeting moment of relief but a long-term journey toward greater emotional resilience, reduced distress, and a sense of freedom from the past. Cognitive defusion is a powerful tool that, when practiced consistently, can fundamentally alter the way you perceive and manage your inner world.

Imagine a time when the memories and thoughts that once felt like heavy chains are now more like passing clouds in the sky. You no longer feel the need to push them away or cling to them; instead, you can watch them drift by with a sense of detachment and curiosity. This newfound ability to observe your thoughts without becoming entangled in them is the cornerstone of emotional resilience. As you become more adept at defusing from your traumatic thoughts, you build a mental and emotional buffer that protects you from the overwhelming impact of distressing memories. This buffer is not a wall that blocks out the world; rather, it's a flexible and adaptive shield that allows you to engage with life more fully, even in the face of challenges.

Over time, the practice of cognitive defusion can lead to a significant reduction in distress. When you no longer identify with your painful thoughts, they lose much of their power to cause you suffering. Instead of feeling like you are living in the past, you can anchor yourself in the present moment, where the richness of life is most vivid. You might find that you are better able to manage stress, anxiety, and other emotional challenges because you have developed the skills to step back and view your thoughts and feelings with a broader perspective. This reduction in distress is not just a temporary reprieve; it is a lasting change that can improve your overall quality of life.

Perhaps one of the most liberating aspects of cognitive defusion is the sense of freedom it brings. Trauma can often leave you feeling trapped, as if your past is a constant shadow that follows you everywhere. But as you practice defusion, you begin to realize that you are not your thoughts, and your thoughts are not you. This realization can be incredibly empowering. You start to see that you have the power to choose how you respond to your thoughts and memories, rather than being at their mercy. This sense of control can be a game-changer, allowing you to pursue your goals and live a more meaningful, fulfilling life. You no longer have to let the past dictate your present or your future.

Consistency is key in this journey. Just as a musician must practice regularly to master an instrument, you must practice cognitive defusion consistently to reap its full benefits. Each time you engage in defusion exercises, you are strengthening your mental muscles and building a more resilient, adaptive mind. The more you practice, the more natural and automatic this process becomes. Over time, you may find that you are better equipped to handle not only your traumatic thoughts but also the everyday challenges that life throws your way.

As you continue on this path, remember that the goal is not to eliminate your thoughts or memories but to change your relationship with them. By practicing cognitive defusion, you are learning to live with your past in a way that no longer holds you back. You are reclaiming your life, one mindful moment at a time. With each step, you are moving closer to a future where you are in control, where your past is a part of your story but not the whole of it. This is a journey worth taking, and the rewards are profound and lasting.

Chapter 5

Allowing Space for Difficult Emotions

"Pain is inevitable. Suffering is optional."
Haruki Murakami

Healing from trauma, one of the most profound and transformative steps you can take is to embrace the concept of emotional expansion. This chapter is about creating a safe and compassionate space within yourself to allow difficult emotions to exist, rather than pushing them away or suppressing them. It's a practice that might seem counterintuitive at first, but it is a cornerstone of Trauma-Focused Acceptance and Commitment Therapy (TF-ACT).

Imagine a river. When a log blocks the flow, the water backs up, creating pressure and potential for flooding. Similarly, when we block or suppress our emotions, they don't disappear; they build up, often leading to more intense and overwhelming feelings. Emotional expansion is like removing the log, allowing the river to flow freely. It's about making room for all your emotions, even the painful ones, and recognizing that they are a natural part of the human experience.

When we talk about emotional expansion, we're not suggesting that you should wallow in your pain or become overwhelmed by it. Instead, we're inviting you to create a space where these emotions can be acknowledged, understood, and eventually, integrated. This process is deeply connected to the principle of acceptance, which is the willingness to experience the present moment as it is, without judgment or resistance.

Acceptance is not about giving up or resigning yourself to a life of suffering. It's about recognizing that your emotions, no matter how difficult, are valid and have a purpose. By accepting your emotions, you are taking the first step towards healing. You are acknowledging that these feelings are a part of your story, but they do not define you. This acceptance is the foundation upon which you can build a life that is meaningful and fulfilling, despite the presence of pain.

Consider this: when you suppress your emotions, you are essentially telling yourself that these feelings are too much to handle, that they are dangerous or wrong. This can lead to a cycle of avoidance and fear, which can exacerbate the trauma. On the other hand, when you allow yourself to feel and accept your emotions, you are sending a powerful message to your mind and body: "I can handle this. I am strong enough to face my pain."

Emotional expansion and acceptance are not one-time events; they are ongoing practices. It's like learning a new language or a musical instrument. The more you practice, the more natural and fluid it becomes. Over time, you'll find that the emotions that once seemed overwhelming become more manageable, and you'll develop a greater sense of resilience.

One of the most significant benefits of emotional expansion is that it can accelerate your recovery from trauma. When you allow yourself to feel and process your emotions, you are giving your mind and body the opportunity to heal. Suppressed emotions can manifest in various ways, such as physical symptoms, anxiety, or depression. By addressing these emotions head-on, you can reduce the likelihood of these symptoms and create a more balanced and healthy life.

Remember, the goal is not to eliminate difficult emotions but to coexist with them in a way that allows you to live a full and meaningful life. This chapter will guide you through practical exercises and strategies to help you practice emotional expansion and acceptance. Each step you take in this process is a step towards reclaiming your life and finding a sense of peace and control.

As you read on, I encourage you to approach this chapter with an open heart and an open mind. This journey is about self-discovery and growth, and it is entirely possible to transform your relationship with your emotions. You are not alone, and you have the strength and resilience to face whatever comes your way.

What Does It Mean to Expand Around Pain?

Emotional expansion in Acceptance and Commitment Therapy (ACT) is a powerful yet often misunderstood concept. It involves making space for difficult emotions rather than trying to avoid or suppress them. This might seem counterintuitive at first, especially when our natural instinct is to push away pain and discomfort. However, the beauty of emotional expansion lies in its transformative potential. By learning to allow these emotions to exist without judgment, we can begin to regain control over our lives in a profound and lasting way.

Imagine you are standing on the edge of a vast, open field. The sky is a mix of stormy clouds and patches of blue, much like the mix of emotions you might feel on any given day. In this field, you come across a small, dark cloud that represents a painful memory or a difficult emotion. Your initial reaction might be to run away from it, to avoid the discomfort it brings. But what if, instead, you decided to stay and watch the cloud? What if you allowed it to be there, without trying to change it or push it away?

This is the essence of emotional expansion. It's about creating a space within yourself where difficult emotions can exist without overwhelming you. It's like standing in that field, acknowledging the presence of the dark cloud, and choosing to let it be. You might feel the weight of the cloud, the sadness or anger it brings, but you don't let it define you. You are more than your emotions, and by making space for them, you can begin to see that.

Let's consider another analogy. Think of your mind as a house, and your emotions as guests. When a difficult emotion knocks on the door, our instinct is often to pretend we're not home or to slam the door in its face. But what if, instead, you opened the door and invited the emotion in, offering it a seat? You might sit with it for a while, listen to what it has to say, and then gently guide it to the door when it's ready to leave. This doesn't mean you have to like the emotion or agree with it; it simply means you're willing to make space for it.

Emotional expansion is not about wallowing in pain or dwelling on negative feelings. It's about recognizing that these emotions are a part of the human experience and that they can teach us valuable lessons. By allowing ourselves to feel these emotions fully, we can better understand their roots and what they are trying to tell us. This understanding can lead to greater self-awareness and, ultimately, to more effective coping strategies.

For example, if you've experienced trauma, you might often feel a sense of fear or anxiety. These emotions are natural responses to your past experiences, and they are valid. By making space for them, you can begin to explore why they arise and what triggers them. You might discover that certain situations or thoughts bring up these feelings, and by understanding this, you can develop strategies to manage them more effectively. You might practice mindfulness techniques, engage in self-compassion, or seek support from a therapist or supportive community.

In the context of trauma-focused ACT, emotional expansion is a crucial step in the healing process. It helps you break the cycle of avoidance and resistance, which can often perpetuate suffering. By learning to accept and make space for your emotions, you can reduce the power they hold over you. This doesn't mean you'll never feel pain again, but it does mean that you can navigate these emotions with greater ease and resilience.

Note that, emotional expansion is a practice, and like any skill, it takes time and patience to develop. Be kind to yourself as you learn to make space for difficult emotions. Each step you take in this journey brings you closer to a life that is more meaningful, fulfilling, and in line with your values.

The Consequences of Emotional Suppression

For many trauma survivors, the instinct to avoid or push away painful feelings is a survival mechanism that initially serves a crucial purpose. However, over time, this avoidance can transform into a double-edged sword, leading to a cascade of psychological and physical consequences that can profoundly impact one's quality of life.

When we suppress our emotions, we are essentially telling our bodies and minds to ignore the signals that are trying to communicate important information. This can start with a seemingly minor act, like brushing off a wave of sadness or anger, but it can quickly spiral into a habitual pattern of emotional avoidance. For trauma survivors, this tendency is often exacerbated by the intensity and complexity of the emotions they experience. The fear of re-experiencing the trauma, the shame associated with certain feelings, or the overwhelming nature of the emotional burden can all drive a person to shut down their emotional responses.

Psychologically, the consequences of suppressing emotions are far-reaching. One of the most immediate effects is an increase in emotional suffering. When we avoid our feelings, they don't simply disappear; instead, they often resurface in more intense and unmanageable forms. This can lead to a cycle of emotional dysregulation, where small triggers can set off disproportionate reactions. For example, a minor disappointment might trigger a deep well of grief or a sudden outburst of anger. Over time, this can erode one's sense of emotional stability and make it increasingly difficult to navigate daily life.

Moreover, the act of suppression itself can be exhausting. It requires a significant amount of mental energy to keep emotions at bay, and this can lead to chronic fatigue, decreased concentration, and a general sense of emotional numbness. Trauma survivors might find themselves feeling disconnected from their own experiences and from the people around them, leading to feelings of isolation and alienation. This emotional disconnection can also manifest as a lack of motivation or a sense of purpose, making it difficult to engage in activities that once brought joy or meaning.

Physically, the consequences of suppressing emotions are equally profound. The body is a sophisticated system that is deeply interconnected with the mind, and emotional suppression can trigger a range of physical responses. Chronic stress, which is often a byproduct of emotional avoidance, can lead to a host of health issues. For instance, the constant activation of the stress response can weaken the immune system, making individuals more susceptible to illnesses. It can also contribute to the development of chronic conditions such as hypertension, heart disease, and diabetes.

Additionally, the physical tension that often accompanies emotional suppression can lead to musculoskeletal problems, such as chronic pain, headaches, and muscle tension. Many trauma survivors find themselves dealing with unexplained physical symptoms that are rooted in their emotional distress. This can create a vicious cycle where physical discomfort leads to more emotional distress, which in turn exacerbates the physical symptoms.

Furthermore, the body's natural healing processes can be impeded by emotional suppression. When we allow ourselves to feel and process our emotions, we activate the parasympathetic nervous system, which helps the body relax and repair. Suppression, on the other hand, keeps the body in a state of high alert, which can interfere with these healing processes. This can lead to slower recovery times from injuries and illnesses, as well as a general sense of physical unease.

In the context of trauma-focused ACT, the importance of addressing emotions cannot be overstated. By learning to expand and accept difficult emotions, individuals can break the cycle of avoidance and begin to heal. This involves creating a safe and supportive space within oneself to acknowledge and validate these feelings, rather than pushing them away. It's about recognizing that emotions, even the most painful ones, are a natural part of the human experience and that they contain valuable information that can guide us toward healing and growth.

Practical Techniques for Emotional Expansion

One of the most powerful tools at your disposal is the practice of emotional expansion. This involves creating a safe and spacious environment within yourself to allow difficult emotions to arise without feeling overwhelmed. It's about learning to sit with these emotions, to observe them without judgment, and to gradually expand your capacity to handle them. Here, we'll explore some actionable steps that can help you practice emotional expansion, making it a regular part of your healing process.

First, let's start with deep breathing exercises. Deep breathing is a simple yet profoundly effective technique that can help you ground yourself in the present moment and create a sense of calm. Find a quiet and comfortable place where you can sit or lie down without distractions. Close your eyes and take a deep breath in through your nose, allowing your belly to rise as you fill your lungs with air. Hold this breath for a few seconds, and then slowly exhale through your mouth, feeling the tension leave your body. As you breathe, try to focus your attention on the sensation of the air moving in and out of your body. If your mind starts to wander, gently bring it back to your breath. This practice helps to regulate your nervous system, reducing the intensity of difficult emotions and creating a sense of inner peace.

Next, consider incorporating body scans into your routine. A body scan is a mindfulness practice that involves systematically focusing your attention on different parts of your body, from your toes all the way up to the top of your head. Start by lying down on your back in a comfortable position. Close your eyes and take a few deep breaths to center yourself. Begin at your toes and slowly move your attention up through your feet, ankles, calves, knees, thighs, and so on. As you focus on each part of your body, notice any sensations, such as tension, warmth, or discomfort. If you encounter a particularly tense area, imagine breathing into that part of your body, allowing the tension to release with each exhale. This practice helps you become more aware of the physical manifestations of your emotions, allowing you to address them more effectively.

Visualization techniques can also be incredibly helpful in creating space for difficult emotions. One effective visualization is the "Expanding the Container" technique. Imagine that your body is a container that holds all your emotions. Visualize this container as a large, flexible vessel that can expand to accommodate whatever you're feeling. As you sit with your emotions, imagine the container expanding to make room for them. If you feel overwhelmed, picture the container growing larger, providing more space for your emotions to exist without overwhelming you. This visualization can help you feel more in control and less threatened by your emotions, allowing you to process them more effectively.

Another powerful visualization is the "Safe Place" technique. Imagine a place where you feel completely safe and at peace. This could be a real place you've visited, or a place you create in your mind. It might be a beach, a forest, a cozy room, or any other environment that brings you comfort. Close your eyes and visualize this place in detail. Notice the sights, sounds, and smells around you. Feel the sense of safety and calm that this place provides. Now, imagine bringing your difficult emotions into this safe place. Picture them as objects or beings that you can observe from a distance. As you sit with these emotions in your safe place, notice how they feel and what they might be trying to tell you. This practice can help you gain new insights into your emotions and reduce the fear and resistance you might feel toward them.

Finally, it's important to approach these practices with a sense of curiosity and self-compassion. Remember that the goal is not to eliminate your difficult emotions but to learn how to be with them in a way that feels manageable and supportive. Each time you practice emotional expansion, you are building your resilience and strengthening your ability to navigate the challenges of life. Be patient with yourself, and celebrate each small step you take on this journey. With time and practice, you'll find that you can sit with your emotions with greater ease and grace, paving the way for a more fulfilling and meaningful life.

Balancing Emotional Expansion with Self-Care

Emotional expansion involves allowing yourself to fully experience and acknowledge your difficult emotions, rather than suppressing or avoiding them. This process is essential for psychological growth and resilience, as it helps you understand and integrate the emotional impact of your trauma. However, it's equally important to recognize when to take a step back and focus on self-soothing and nurturing activities. This balance ensures that you are not overwhelmed and can maintain a sense of stability and well-being.

When you engage in emotional expansion, you open yourself up to the full spectrum of your feelings, including pain, fear, and sadness. This can be incredibly liberating, as it allows you to confront and process the emotions that have been holding you back. It's like peeling back the layers of a complex onion, each layer revealing more about your inner world. However, this process can also be intense and draining. It's important to listen to your body and mind, and to recognize the signs that you need to take a break. These signs might include feeling overwhelmed, exhausted, or emotionally drained. When you notice these signals, it's time to shift your focus to self-care.

Self-care is not a luxury; it is a necessity. It involves activities and practices that help you recharge and maintain your emotional and physical health. These can range from simple acts like taking a warm bath, going for a walk in nature, or practicing deep breathing exercises, to more structured activities like yoga, meditation, or journaling. The key is to find what works best for you and to make it a regular part of your routine. Self-care is about nurturing yourself and creating a safe space where you can feel calm and centered.

Balancing emotional expansion with self-care is like dancing a delicate but powerful dance. On one hand, you are facing your deepest fears and challenges, which can be daunting and exhausting. On the other hand, you are taking care of yourself, which provides the strength and resilience needed to continue this journey. It's important to approach this balance with self-compassion. Be kind to yourself when you need to step back and take a break. Recognize that taking care of yourself is not a sign of weakness, but a sign of strength and wisdom.

One way to achieve this balance is to set clear boundaries and create a self-care plan. This plan can include specific activities you can turn to when you feel overwhelmed. For example, you might decide to spend 10 minutes each day practicing mindfulness, or to take a short walk after a particularly challenging session of emotional exploration. By having a plan in place, you can ensure that you are consistently taking care of yourself, even when you are deeply engaged in the process of emotional expansion.

Another important aspect of this balance is learning to recognize and validate your emotions. When you feel the urge to pull back, don't judge yourself for it. Instead, acknowledge that it's okay to feel this way and that taking a break is a healthy and necessary part of the healing process. This validation can help you feel more in control and less overwhelmed. It's also helpful to have a support system in place, whether it's friends, family, or a therapist, who can provide encouragement and guidance as you navigate this balance.

Ultimately, the goal is to create a sustainable and compassionate approach to healing. By integrating emotional expansion with healthy self-care practices, you can build the resilience and inner strength needed to face your trauma and move forward with a sense of purpose and fulfillment. This balance is not about avoiding difficult emotions but about learning to manage them in a way that promotes growth and well-being. As you continue on this journey, remember that you are not alone, and that each step you take, no matter how small, is a step toward a more meaningful and fulfilling life.

How Emotional Expansion Leads to Healing

Emotional expansion is a powerful practice that can transform the way trauma survivors process and integrate their difficult experiences, ultimately leading to lasting emotional healing. Unlike the common instinct to avoid or suppress painful emotions, expansion involves creating a safe and spacious environment within oneself to fully experience and acknowledge these emotions. This process is not about drowning in the pain but rather about learning to swim with it, allowing it to flow through you without being overwhelmed.

Consider the story of Sarah, a trauma survivor who had been struggling with the aftermath of a violent assault for years. Initially, Sarah found herself in a constant state of hypervigilance, her mind frequently replaying the traumatic event. She tried various coping mechanisms, from numbing herself with substances to avoiding any triggers that might bring back the memories. However, these strategies only provided temporary relief and often left her feeling more isolated and disconnected from her life.

One day, Sarah decided to seek help and began working with a therapist who specialized in Trauma-Focused Acceptance and Commitment Therapy (TF-ACT). Her therapist introduced her to the concept of emotional expansion. At first, Sarah was skeptical. How could facing her fears and pain possibly help her heal? But she was willing to try.

The therapist guided Sarah through a series of exercises designed to help her create space for her emotions. They started with simple mindfulness practices, where Sarah learned to observe her thoughts and feelings without judgment. She was encouraged to notice the physical sensations associated with her emotions, such as the tightness in her chest or the knot in her stomach, and to breathe into these sensations. Over time, Sarah began to see that her emotions, while intense, were not permanent. They came and went like waves in the ocean, and she could ride them out without being swept away.

As Sarah became more comfortable with this practice, her therapist introduced more advanced techniques, such as the "Leaves on a Stream" exercise. In this visualization, Sarah imagined her thoughts and emotions as leaves floating down a stream. She watched them pass by without trying to hold onto them or push them away. This exercise helped Sarah develop a sense of detachment from her emotions, allowing her to see them as transient experiences rather than defining aspects of her identity.

Sarah also practiced self-compassion, a crucial component of emotional expansion. She learned to treat herself with the same kindness and understanding she would offer a friend going through a difficult time. This shift in perspective helped her to be more gentle with herself and to recognize that her pain was a natural response to her trauma. She began to see that her emotions were valid and worthy of attention, rather than something to be feared or suppressed.

Through these practices, Sarah gradually found that her emotional landscape was changing. The intensity of her anxiety and fear began to diminish, and she started to experience moments of peace and clarity. She realized that by allowing herself to fully experience her emotions, she was able to process and integrate them in a way that was healing and transformative. Instead of being controlled by her past, she was beginning to reclaim her present and future.

The practice of emotional expansion is not easy, and it requires courage and commitment. However, the rewards are profound. By creating space for difficult emotions, trauma survivors like Sarah can break free from the cycle of avoidance and repression. They can learn to live with their pain without being dominated by it, and they can rediscover a sense of purpose and meaning in their lives. This journey is not about erasing the past but about finding a way to move forward, even with the scars of trauma.

As Sarah's story illustrates, emotional expansion is a powerful tool for healing. It teaches us that our emotions, no matter how painful, are not our enemies. By facing them with openness and compassion, we can find the strength to heal and to live a more fulfilling, authentic life. The path may be challenging, but the destination is one of resilience, growth, and renewed hope.

Chapter 6

Breaking Free from the Past

*"Trauma is a fact of life. It does not, however, have
to be a life sentence."*
Bessel van der Kolk, M.D.

In the journey of trauma recovery, one of the most powerful yet often overlooked tools is the ability to stay present. Trauma has a unique way of anchoring us in the past, making it feel as though the painful events that once occurred are still happening now. The echoes of the past can be so loud that they drown out the present, leaving us feeling trapped and powerless. But what if I told you that the key to breaking free from this cycle lies in the here and now?

Imagine a tree rooted deeply in the earth, its branches reaching toward the sky. The roots represent our past—strong, sometimes tangled, but essential for stability. The branches symbolize the present, reaching out to the future, absorbing sunlight, and growing. Trauma can feel like a storm that threatens to uproot the tree, but by grounding ourselves in the present, we can weather the storm and continue to grow. This chapter will guide you through the process of connecting with the present moment, a practice that is not just a coping mechanism but a transformative journey toward healing and empowerment.

Trauma has a way of hijacking our minds, pulling us back into the moments of pain and fear. It's as if a part of us is forever stuck in the past, reliving the trauma over and over again. This constant mental time travel can be exhausting, leaving us feeling drained and disconnected from the world around us. The good news is that the present moment is always available to us, a safe haven where we can find peace and clarity.

Mindfulness, the practice of being fully present and engaged in the moment, is a powerful tool in trauma recovery. It allows us to observe our thoughts and emotions without judgment, to recognize that we are not our thoughts, and to choose how we want to respond to them. When we are mindful, we can acknowledge the pain of the past without being consumed by it. We can see that our experiences, while significant, do not define us. Instead, they are part of a larger story, one that includes our resilience, our growth, and our capacity for joy.

Think of mindfulness as a bridge between the past and the present. By crossing this bridge, we can leave the weight of the past behind and step into a more vibrant, fulfilling life. It's not about forgetting what happened or pretending it didn't matter; it's about integrating those experiences into our lives in a way that allows us to move forward with purpose and intention.

In this chapter, we will explore practical techniques for staying present, such as mindfulness meditation, grounding exercises, and sensory awareness. These tools are designed to help you reconnect with your body, your environment, and your inner self. By doing so, you will begin to build a stronger, more resilient foundation for your recovery. You will learn to recognize the signs that you are being pulled into the past and develop strategies to gently guide yourself back to the present.

The Power of the Present Moment in Trauma Recovery

When individuals are able to stay mindful and fully engaged in the here and now, they can begin to break free from the emotional grip of the past. This is not to say that the past ceases to exist or that its impact is erased; rather, it means that the present becomes a sanctuary where one can find a sense of peace and control, even amidst the echoes of past trauma.

Mindfulness, at its core, is the practice of being fully present and engaged in the current moment, without judgment. It involves observing one's thoughts, feelings, and bodily sensations with a curious and non-reactive awareness. For those who have experienced trauma, this practice can be particularly transformative. Trauma often leaves individuals feeling stuck in a loop of painful memories and emotions, constantly reliving the past and fearing the future. Mindfulness helps to anchor them in the present, providing a much-needed respite from the relentless pull of those traumatic experiences.

Scientific research has consistently supported the benefits of mindfulness in trauma recovery. A study published in the *Journal of Traumatic Stress* found that mindfulness-based interventions significantly reduced symptoms of post-traumatic stress disorder (PTSD) in individuals who had experienced various forms of trauma. The research highlighted that mindfulness practices, such as mindful breathing and body scans, helped participants develop a greater sense of emotional regulation and reduced the frequency and intensity of intrusive thoughts and flashbacks.

Another study in the *Clinical Psychology Review* explored the neural mechanisms underlying the effects of mindfulness on trauma. The findings indicated that regular mindfulness practice can lead to changes in brain regions associated with emotion regulation, such as the prefrontal cortex and the amygdala. These changes contribute to a more balanced and resilient emotional state, making it easier for individuals to manage the intense emotions that often accompany trauma.

Moreover, mindfulness helps individuals develop a more compassionate and accepting attitude toward themselves and their experiences. Trauma can often breed self-blame and self-criticism, creating a cycle of negative self-talk that further exacerbates emotional distress. By cultivating mindfulness, individuals can learn to observe their thoughts and feelings with kindness and understanding, rather than judgment. This shift in perspective can be profoundly healing, allowing them to approach their past with greater clarity and less emotional reactivity.

In the context of Trauma-Focused Acceptance and Commitment Therapy (TF-ACT), mindfulness plays a crucial role in helping individuals develop psychological flexibility. Psychological flexibility is the ability to be present, open up to experiences, and take effective action guided by personal values. For those who have experienced trauma, this flexibility is essential for navigating the complex emotions and thoughts that arise. Mindfulness practices within TF-ACT are designed to enhance this flexibility, enabling individuals to stay grounded in the present moment and make choices that align with their values, rather than being driven by past trauma.

In practical terms, mindfulness can be integrated into daily life through simple yet powerful practices. For example, taking a few minutes each day to focus on the breath, noticing the sensations of each inhale and exhale, can help anchor one in the present. Engaging fully in activities, whether it's cooking, walking, or spending time with loved ones, can also foster a sense of presence and connection. Over time, these practices can become a natural part of one's routine, providing a consistent source of stability and peace.

Ultimately, the therapeutic power of the present moment lies in its ability to offer a refuge from the past. By cultivating mindfulness, individuals can learn to live more fully in the here and now, breaking free from the emotional chains of trauma and reclaiming their lives. This journey is not always easy, but with patience, practice, and a supportive approach, it is a path that can lead to profound healing and transformation.

Recognizing When You're Not Present

Trauma has a way of pulling us back into the past or catapulting us into an anxious future, making it difficult to engage with the here and now. This disconnection can manifest in various ways, and understanding these signs is the first step toward reclaiming your present.

When you find yourself ruminating on past trauma, it can feel like you are reliving the event over and over again. The memories might be vivid, accompanied by intense emotions and physical sensations. You might notice your heart rate increasing, your breath becoming shallow, or a knot forming in your stomach. These physical reactions are your body's way of signaling that you are in a state of distress, even though the threat is not present. It's important to acknowledge these feelings without judgment. Recognize that your mind is trying to make sense of a painful experience, but it's also keeping you from fully engaging with the present.

Anxiety about the future can also pull you out of the present moment. You might find yourself constantly worrying about what might happen, imagining worst-case scenarios, or feeling overwhelmed by the uncertainty of life. This type of thinking can be paralyzing, making it hard to focus on the tasks at hand. Signs of future-oriented anxiety include a racing mind, difficulty sleeping, and a sense of restlessness. You might feel like you need to constantly be prepared for something that hasn't even happened yet. This perpetual state of vigilance can be exhausting and can prevent you from enjoying the present.

Dissociation is another common way that trauma can manifest, and it can be more subtle than the other signs. Dissociation is a coping mechanism that your mind uses to distance itself from overwhelming experiences. You might feel disconnected from your body, as if you are watching yourself from a distance. Time can feel distorted, and you might have difficulty recalling recent events. Some people describe it as feeling "numb" or "spaced out." If you notice these symptoms, it's important to recognize that your mind is trying to protect you from pain, but it's also keeping you from fully experiencing life.

Distraction is a more everyday form of disconnection, but it can be just as significant. You might find yourself constantly checking your phone, mindlessly scrolling through social media, or engaging in other activities that keep your mind occupied. While these distractions can provide temporary relief, they can also prevent you from addressing the underlying issues. If you find that you are frequently avoiding moments of quiet or solitude, it might be a sign that you are using distractions to avoid difficult thoughts and emotions.

The key to breaking free from these patterns is to develop a greater awareness of your internal experiences. Mindfulness practices, such as deep breathing, grounding techniques, and body scans, can help you reconnect with the present moment. When you notice that you are ruminating on the past or worrying about the future, gently bring your attention back to your breath. Feel the sensation of the air moving in and out of your body, and allow yourself to be fully present in that moment.

If you find yourself dissociating, try to engage your senses. Notice the colors around you, the sounds you can hear, and the textures you can feel. Grounding yourself in the physical world can help you feel more connected and present.

For distractions, consider setting aside specific times for activities that you enjoy, but also make time for moments of reflection and stillness. Create a safe space where you can sit quietly and simply be with your thoughts and feelings. It's okay to feel uncomfortable at first, but with practice, you will become more comfortable with the present moment.

Mindfulness Practices for Staying Grounded

These practices help you anchor yourself in the here and now, reducing the hold that painful memories and emotions may have on your daily life. Let's explore some practical and encouraging exercises that you can easily integrate into your routine.

Mindful breathing is a foundational practice that can be done anywhere, at any time. Start by finding a comfortable and quiet spot where you can sit or lie down. Close your eyes gently and bring your attention to your breath. Notice the sensation of the air as it enters and leaves your nostrils or the rise and fall of your chest. If your mind wanders, which it will, gently guide it back to the breath without judgment. As you inhale, imagine drawing in peace and calm. As you exhale, imagine releasing any tension or stress. This simple act of focusing on your breath can be a powerful anchor, helping you to stay grounded and centered. You can practice this for just a few minutes or extend it to longer periods as you become more comfortable.

Body awareness is another essential practice that can help you connect with the present moment. Begin by sitting in a comfortable position or lying down. Close your eyes and take a few deep breaths to settle in. Start at the top of your head and slowly scan down through your body, noticing any sensations, tensions, or areas of relaxation. As you move through each part—your forehead, cheeks, jaw, neck, shoulders, arms, hands, chest, abdomen, hips, legs, and feet—breathe into any areas of tension and imagine the tension dissolving with each exhale. If you find a particularly tense area, you can gently tense and then release that muscle group. This practice helps you become more attuned to your body's signals and can reduce physical and emotional stress.

Sensory focus techniques are also incredibly effective for grounding yourself in the present. One simple exercise is the 5-4-3-2-1 method. Start by identifying five things you can see around you. They could be anything—a book, a plant, a piece of furniture. Next, find four things you can touch. You might touch the fabric of your clothing, the surface of a table, or the ground beneath your feet. Then, listen for three sounds. It could be the hum of a refrigerator, the rustle of leaves, or the distant sound of traffic. Next, identify two things you can smell. This might be the scent of a candle, the aroma of coffee, or the fresh air. Finally, find one thing you can taste. You might take a sip of water, a bite of a snack, or simply notice the taste in your mouth. This exercise helps you engage all your senses and brings you fully into the present moment.

Another sensory focus technique is the "raisin exercise," which is often used in mindfulness training. Take a raisin or any small piece of food. Hold it in your hand and really look at it, noticing its color, texture, and shape. Bring it to your nose and smell it, noting any aromas. Place it in your mouth but don't chew yet. Feel its texture with your tongue and notice any initial tastes. When you're ready, start to chew slowly, savoring the experience. Pay attention to the flavors, the texture, and the sensations in your mouth. This exercise can be done with any food and helps you cultivate a sense of presence and appreciation for the simple things in life.

Incorporating these mindfulness exercises into your daily routine can be a transformative practice. Whether you choose to start your day with a few minutes of mindful breathing, take a sensory focus break during a stressful moment, or end your day with a body awareness scan, these practices can help you build a stronger connection with the present moment. By doing so, you can reduce the impact of past traumas and create a more fulfilling and meaningful life.

Coping with Flashbacks and Intrusive Thoughts in the Present

This practice involves fully engaging with the here and now, allowing you to break free from the grip of painful memories and intrusive thoughts. When a flashback or intrusive thought strikes, it can feel as though you are reliving the trauma all over again. However, by grounding yourself in the present, you can regain a sense of control and safety. Here's how you can use present-moment awareness to cope with these distressing moments.

First, take a deep breath. Inhale slowly through your nose, feeling the air fill your lungs, and then exhale gently through your mouth. This simple act of breathing can serve as an anchor, bringing your focus back to the present. As you breathe, try to notice the sensation of the air moving in and out of your body. Feel the rise and fall of your chest, the coolness of the air as it enters your nostrils, and the warmth as it leaves your mouth. This mindful breathing can help calm your nervous system and reduce the intensity of the flashback.

Next, engage your senses. Look around you and identify five things you can see. Notice the colors, shapes, and textures of these objects. Listen carefully and identify four sounds in your environment. It could be the hum of a fan, the rustling of leaves, or the distant sound of traffic. Touch three things around you and feel their textures. Perhaps the smooth surface of a table, the soft fabric of a pillow, or the rough bark of a tree. Taste two things, even if it's just the flavor lingering in your mouth from your last meal. Finally, smell one thing. It could be the scent of a flower, the aroma of coffee, or the fresh air outside. By focusing on your senses, you can anchor yourself in the present and distance yourself from the trauma.

Another effective technique is to engage in a physical activity that requires your full attention. This could be something as simple as walking, where you focus on the sensation of your feet touching the ground with each step. Feel the ground beneath you, the rhythm of your steps, and the movement of your body. Alternatively, you could try a more structured activity like yoga or tai chi, which combine movement with mindfulness. These activities can help you reconnect with your body and the present moment, reducing the power of intrusive thoughts.

Mindful movement can also be a powerful tool. Try a simple exercise like the "5-4-3-2-1" grounding technique. Start by finding a comfortable position, either sitting or standing. Close your eyes and take a deep breath. As you exhale, visualize yourself becoming more grounded and centered. Now, open your eyes and begin to engage your senses. Notice five things you can see, four things you can touch, three things you can hear, two things you can smell, and one thing you can taste. This technique can be particularly helpful in moments of high distress, as it provides a structured and calming way to reconnect with the present.

It's also important to acknowledge and validate your feelings. When a flashback or intrusive thought occurs, it's natural to feel overwhelmed. Instead of pushing these feelings away, try to observe them with curiosity and compassion. You might say to yourself, "I'm feeling scared right now, and that's okay. This is a normal response to what I've been through." By acknowledging your emotions, you can create some distance between yourself and the trauma, allowing you to respond more calmly and effectively.

Finally, consider creating a "safe space" for yourself. This can be a physical place in your home where you feel secure and comfortable, or it can be an imaginary space in your mind. When you feel a flashback coming on, visualize yourself in this safe space. Imagine the details of this place—the colors, the sounds, the smells, and the sensations. Feel the sense of calm and safety that this space brings you. You can return to this safe space whenever you need a moment of respite from the intensity of your thoughts and emotions.

By practicing these grounding techniques, you can learn to manage the distressing symptoms of trauma more effectively. Remember, it's a process, and it's okay to take it one step at a time. With patience and practice, you can develop a stronger connection with the present moment and find the resilience to move forward in your healing journey.

Building a Routine of Present-Moment Awareness

Building a daily routine around present-moment awareness is a transformative practice that can profoundly impact your journey of healing and growth. When you are deeply connected to the present, you are less likely to be pulled into the painful memories of the past or the anxieties of the future. This connection allows you to experience life more fully and authentically, fostering a sense of peace and control that might have seemed unattainable before.

One of the most effective ways to integrate present-moment awareness into your daily life is through mindfulness practices. These practices are not about adding more tasks to your to-do list but rather about infusing your existing activities with a sense of purpose and presence. For instance, when you sit down for a meal, try to engage all your senses. Notice the colors and textures of the food, the aroma that fills the air, and the flavors that dance on your tongue. Chew slowly and savor each bite, allowing yourself to be fully present in the experience. This simple act can transform a routine meal into a mindful practice that grounds you in the here and now.

Similarly, when you take a walk, whether it's a short stroll around your neighborhood or a longer hike in nature, focus on the sensations of your body. Feel the ground beneath your feet, the breeze on your skin, and the sounds of the environment around you. Instead of letting your mind wander to past events or future worries, bring your attention back to the present moment. This practice can help you cultivate a deeper sense of connection with the world around you, reducing the hold that traumatic memories might have on your thoughts.

In conversations, too, you can practice mindfulness. When you are speaking with someone, give them your full attention. Listen actively, without planning your next response or getting lost in your own thoughts. Notice the tone of their voice, the expressions on their face, and the emotions they are conveying. By being fully present in your interactions, you not only deepen your connections with others but also create a space where you can process and manage your own emotions more effectively.

Another powerful way to build present-moment awareness is through regular mindfulness meditation. Even a few minutes each day can make a significant difference. Find a quiet space where you can sit comfortably and close your eyes. Focus on your breath, feeling the air as it enters and leaves your body. When your mind starts to wander, gently bring it back to your breath. Over time, this practice will train your mind to stay more focused and less reactive to past traumas.

Incorporating these mindfulness practices into your daily routine is not about achieving perfection but about building a habit of presence. It's about making a commitment to yourself to live more fully in the moments that matter. As you continue to practice, you will likely notice a shift in how you experience life. You might find that the grip of the past loosens, and you are better able to navigate the challenges of the present with a sense of resilience and grace. Remember, the journey of healing is a continuous process, and each step you take towards present-moment awareness is a step towards reclaiming your life.

Chapter 7

The Observing Self – Cultivating a Balanced Perspective on Trauma

*"Between stimulus and response, there is a space. In
that space is our power to choose our response. In our
response lies our growth and our freedom."*
Viktor E. Frankl

In the journey of trauma recovery, one of the most powerful tools at your disposal is the concept of the observing self. This chapter will guide you through the process of cultivating an inner perspective that allows you to observe your thoughts and emotions without becoming overwhelmed by them. By developing this skill, you can create a space between your traumatic experiences and your reactions, giving you the freedom to choose how you respond to the world around you.

Imagine for a moment that your mind is a vast, expansive landscape. In this landscape, there are many different terrains: the rugged mountains of intense emotions, the deep valleys of painful memories, and the serene lakes of calm and peace. The observing self is like a bird that can soar above this landscape, seeing everything from a higher vantage point. From this elevated perspective, you can observe the different parts of your inner world without getting caught up in the tumult below.

When you cultivate the observing self, you are not trying to eliminate or suppress your thoughts and emotions. Instead, you are learning to hold them with a gentle, non-judgmental awareness. This shift in perspective can be transformative. It allows you to recognize that your thoughts and emotions are just passing phenomena, like clouds moving across the sky. They are not permanent fixtures of who you are. By observing them from a distance, you can gain a more balanced and nuanced understanding of your experiences.

One of the key benefits of the observing self is that it helps you break the cycle of automatic reactivity. Trauma can create deep grooves in your mind, making it easy to fall into patterns of fear, anger, or despair. When you are caught in these patterns, it can feel like you are on a runaway train, with no control over your destination. The observing self gives you the power to step off that train and choose a different path. It allows you to pause, reflect, and respond in ways that are aligned with your values and goals.

Cultivating the observing self is not always easy. It requires practice and patience. It involves learning to sit with discomfort, to be present with your thoughts and emotions without trying to change them. This can be challenging, especially when those thoughts and emotions are painful or distressing. But with time and dedication, you can develop the skills to observe your inner world with greater clarity and compassion.

In this chapter, we will explore various techniques and exercises that can help you strengthen your observing self. We will delve into mindfulness practices, such as meditation and breathing exercises, that can enhance your ability to stay present and aware. We will also discuss the importance of self-compassion and how it can support you in your journey of observation. By the end of this chapter, you will have a toolkit of strategies that you can use to cultivate a balanced perspective on your trauma and move forward with greater resilience and purpose.

What Is the Observing Self?

In the realm of Acceptance and Commitment Therapy (ACT), the concept of the observing self is a cornerstone that offers a profound shift in perspective for individuals grappling with the aftermath of trauma. The observing self, also known as the pure self or the self as context, is the part of you that is aware and present, the silent witness to your thoughts, feelings, and experiences. It is the part of you that remains constant, even as everything around you and within you changes. This concept is not about denying or escaping from your thoughts and emotions; rather, it is about recognizing that you are more than just the sum of your internal experiences.

To truly understand the observing self, imagine a vast sky. The sky remains unchanged, regardless of the weather. Clouds may come and go—some dark and stormy, others bright and sunny—but the sky itself is always there, a constant backdrop to the ever-changing conditions. In the same way, your observing self is the sky, and your thoughts and feelings are the clouds. When you cultivate the ability to observe your thoughts and feelings from this vantage point, you begin to see that these mental and emotional states are transient, like passing clouds. They do not define who you are at your core.

This shift in perspective is incredibly empowering. It allows you to step back from the intense emotional storms that trauma can create, to see them for what they are: just thoughts and feelings. By recognizing that you are the observer of these experiences, you can create a space between yourself and your thoughts, a space where you can choose how to respond rather than react. This is crucial in the context of trauma, where the automatic, reactive patterns of the mind can often lead to feelings of helplessness and loss of control.

For example, consider a person who has experienced a traumatic event and frequently has intrusive thoughts and flashbacks. Without the concept of the observing self, this person might feel overwhelmed, believing that these thoughts and feelings are an inseparable part of their identity. However, by cultivating the observing self, they can learn to say, "I am having the thought that I am unsafe," rather than "I am unsafe." This subtle but powerful shift in language and perspective helps to separate the person from the content of their thoughts, reducing the grip that these thoughts have on their emotional well-being.

Moreover, the observing self is not just about detaching from negative thoughts and feelings; it is also about connecting with the present moment and the richness of life. When you are able to observe your thoughts and feelings without judgment, you can more easily engage with the world around you. You can appreciate the beauty of a sunset, the warmth of a friend's embrace, or the simple joy of a good meal, even in the face of difficult internal experiences. This ability to be present and engaged is a key aspect of psychological flexibility, which is central to the principles of ACT.

In the context of trauma, the observing self is a powerful tool for regaining a sense of control and agency. It helps individuals to recognize that they are not their trauma, but the resilient, aware beings who have the capacity to heal and grow. By cultivating this perspective, you can learn to live a more meaningful and fulfilling life, one where you are not defined by your past but are free to create a future that aligns with your values and aspirations.

The Role of the Observing Self in Trauma Recovery

The observing self is a part of you that is always present, detached, and aware. It is the part of you that can step back and observe your thoughts, emotions, and physical sensations without judgment. By cultivating this observing self, you can gain a sense of distance from your traumatic memories and emotional pain, which can significantly reduce your emotional reactivity.

Imagine, for a moment, that you are standing at the edge of a river. The river represents your stream of consciousness, where thoughts, emotions, and memories flow by like the water. The observing self is you, standing on the bank, watching the river flow. You can see the water, feel the breeze, and hear the sounds, but you are not the water itself. You are the observer, separate from the current. This perspective allows you to witness your experiences without being swept away by them.

For trauma survivors, this can be life-changing. When a traumatic memory arises, it often comes with a surge of intense emotions—fear, anger, sadness, or even numbness. These emotions can feel overwhelming, as if they are defining who you are. However, by accessing the observing self, you can create a mental space between you and the memory. You can acknowledge the memory and the emotions it brings, but you can also remind yourself that these are just experiences, not who you are at your core.

For example, let's say you are triggered by a sound that reminds you of a traumatic event. Instead of immediately reacting with fear or panic, you can take a deep breath and step into the role of the observing self. You might say to yourself, "I notice that I am feeling afraid right now. I hear the sound, and it reminds me of the past. But I am here, in the present, and I am safe." This simple act of observation can help you ground yourself in the present moment, reducing the intensity of the emotional reaction.

Another way the observing self can help is by fostering a sense of curiosity. When you are curious about your experiences, you are less likely to judge them harshly. You can ask yourself questions like, "What is this emotion trying to tell me?" or "What can I learn from this memory?" This curiosity can transform your relationship with your trauma. Instead of seeing your memories as threats, you can view them as opportunities for growth and understanding.

For instance, if you find yourself feeling angry about a past betrayal, you might initially react with a desire to lash out or withdraw. But by stepping into the observing self, you can explore the anger with curiosity. You might realize that the anger is a protective mechanism, a way of shielding yourself from vulnerability. This insight can lead to a deeper understanding of your own needs and boundaries, allowing you to make choices that are aligned with your values and well-being.

The observing self also helps in managing the physical symptoms of trauma. Trauma can manifest in the body as tension, pain, or discomfort. By observing these sensations without judgment, you can begin to release the physical tension. You might notice that your shoulders are tense and consciously relax them, or that your breath is shallow and take deep, calming breaths. This practice of mindfulness can reduce the physical manifestations of trauma, making it easier to manage the emotional aspects.

Observing self is a powerful ally in your healing journey. It allows you to step back from the chaos of your thoughts and emotions, to see them for what they are—

passing experiences. By cultivating this perspective, you can gain a sense of control over your life, reducing the impact of traumatic memories and emotional pain. This shift in perspective is not about denying your experiences or pushing them away; it is about creating a space where you can process them with greater clarity and compassion. As you continue to practice accessing the observing self, you will find that you can navigate the challenges of trauma with greater ease and resilience.

Techniques for Accessing the Observing Self

This aspect of your consciousness allows you to step back and view your thoughts and emotions from a distance, much like a bird observing the landscape from high above. By cultivating this perspective, you can gain a balanced and more objective view of your experiences, which is essential for managing overwhelming thoughts and emotions. Here are some practical techniques to help you access and strengthen your observing self.

Meditation is a foundational practice for developing the observing self. Find a quiet, comfortable place where you can sit or lie down without distractions. Close your eyes and take a few deep breaths, allowing your body to relax. As you breathe, bring your attention to the present moment. Notice the sensations in your body, the sounds around you, and the feelings that arise. When thoughts or emotions come up, observe them without judgment.

Imagine them as clouds passing through the sky of your mind. Acknowledge their presence, but do not engage with them. Simply watch them as they come and go. This practice of non-attachment helps you develop the ability to observe your inner world without being swept away by it.

Mindfulness exercises can also be incredibly effective in cultivating the observing self. One simple yet powerful exercise is the "Three-Minute Breathing Space." This technique involves three steps: focusing on your breath, expanding your awareness to your body, and then broadening your attention to include your surroundings. Start by bringing your attention to your breath. Notice the sensation of the air entering and leaving your nostrils, or the rise and fall of your chest. After a minute, expand your awareness to include your entire body. Notice any sensations, tensions, or areas of discomfort. Finally, broaden your attention to include the environment around you. Notice the sounds, smells, and any other sensory inputs. This exercise helps you ground yourself in the present moment and observe your experience with greater clarity.

Visualization can be another powerful tool for accessing the observing self. Imagine yourself standing at the edge of a river, and each thought or emotion is a leaf floating on the water. As you stand there, watch the leaves as they drift by. Some may be large and turbulent, while others are small and calm. Observe each leaf without trying to change its course or hold onto it. Allow them to flow naturally, recognizing that they are just passing phenomena. This visualization helps you develop a sense of detachment from your thoughts and emotions, allowing you to see them as temporary and not defining aspects of who you are.

Another technique is the "Self-As-Context" exercise. This involves imagining yourself in a series of different contexts, such as a child, a teenager, and an adult. As you visualize each stage, notice how your thoughts, feelings, and behaviors have changed over time. Despite these changes, there is a constant aspect of you that has remained the same—the observing self. This exercise helps you recognize that while your experiences and reactions may vary, there is a core part of you that is stable and unchanging. This awareness can provide a sense of continuity and stability, which is particularly valuable when navigating the challenges of trauma.

Finally, journaling can be a powerful way to cultivate the observing self. Set aside a few minutes each day to write down your thoughts and feelings. As you write, try to observe your inner dialogue with curiosity and without judgment. Notice any patterns or recurring themes. Reflect on how your thoughts and emotions are influencing your actions and decisions. By putting your experiences into words, you can gain a clearer perspective and develop a deeper understanding of your inner world. This practice can also help you identify areas where you might need to apply the principles of acceptance and commitment.

By incorporating these practices into your daily life, you can gradually strengthen your observing self and develop a more balanced and grounded perspective on your trauma. Remember, the goal is not to eliminate your thoughts and emotions but to learn how to coexist with them in a way that supports your well-being and helps you lead a meaningful, fulfilling life.

Cultivating Self-Compassion Through the Observing Self

Developing the observing self is a profound and transformative practice that can significantly enhance self-compassion, especially for those who have experienced trauma. When we cultivate the observing self, we learn to step back from our immediate experiences and view them with a broader, more balanced perspective. This shift in perspective is not about denying or suppressing our emotions but about understanding them with greater clarity and kindness.

Imagine, for a moment, that you are standing on a hilltop, looking down at a valley. In this valley, you see a river that represents your thoughts and emotions. Sometimes, the river is calm and peaceful, and other times, it is turbulent and chaotic. When we are caught up in the river, it can feel overwhelming and all-consuming. But when we step back and observe the river from the hilltop, we gain a different vantage point. We can see the river for what it is—a natural part of the landscape, ebbing and flowing, but not defining the entire valley.

For trauma survivors, this observing self can be a powerful tool for self-compassion. When we are in the thick of difficult emotions—fear, anger, grief, or shame— it can feel as though these emotions are who we are. But the observing self reminds us that these emotions are just one part of our experience, and they do not define our entire being. By cultivating this perspective, we can begin to treat ourselves with the same kindness and understanding that we might offer to a dear friend.

Think about a time when a friend was going through a tough situation. Chances are, you didn't judge them harshly or tell them to just get over it. Instead, you probably listened with empathy, offered words of comfort, and reminded them that they are more than their current struggles. The observing self allows us to do the same for ourselves. When we observe our emotions from a distance, we can acknowledge them without judgment and respond with compassion.

For example, if you are feeling overwhelmed by a traumatic memory, the observing self might say, "I notice that I am feeling overwhelmed right now. This is a natural response to what I have experienced, and it is okay to feel this way." By acknowledging your emotions in this way, you are showing yourself the same kindness and understanding that you would offer to someone you care about. This practice can help you break the cycle of self-criticism and develop a more supportive inner dialogue.

Moreover, the observing self can help you recognize that your emotions are temporary and will pass. Just as the river in the valley changes with the seasons, your emotions will ebb and flow over time. By observing this process, you can develop a sense of resilience and patience. You can remind yourself that, no matter how difficult the current moment may be, it is not permanent. This perspective can provide a sense of hope and comfort, allowing you to navigate your emotions with greater ease.

In essence, the observing self is a compassionate witness to your experiences. It helps you see that you are more than your thoughts and emotions, and that you have the capacity to treat yourself with kindness and understanding. By cultivating this perspective, you can create a more balanced and nurturing relationship with yourself, even in the face of challenging emotions. This practice is a cornerstone of Trauma-Focused ACT, as it empowers you to regain control of your life and move forward with a sense of purpose and well-being.

The Long-Term Benefits of a Balanced Perspective

Cultivating the observing self is a transformative practice that can profoundly impact your emotional balance and resilience over the long term. When you develop the ability to step back and observe your thoughts and emotions from a distance, you gain a powerful tool for managing the often overwhelming aftermath of trauma. This perspective allows you to see your experiences not as defining aspects of your identity but as transient events that you can observe and eventually let go of.

Imagine a vast, clear sky. The sky represents your observing self, a constant, unchanging part of you that exists beyond the clouds of your thoughts and emotions. The clouds, much like your thoughts and feelings, come and go. Some are dark and stormy, while others are light and fluffy. By cultivating the observing self, you learn to watch these clouds without getting caught up in their turbulence. This detachment doesn't mean you ignore your emotions; rather, it means you can acknowledge them, understand their role, and choose how to respond rather than react impulsively.

For example, consider someone who has experienced a traumatic event, such as a car accident. The memories and emotions associated with that event can be intense and overwhelming. Without the observing self, these feelings might dominate their life, leading to anxiety, depression, and a sense of helplessness. However, by practicing the observing self, they can step back and see these emotions as just one part of their experience. They might say to themselves, "I am feeling anxious right now, but that doesn't mean I am anxiety. I can observe this feeling, understand where it comes from, and choose to take a deep breath, ground myself, and move forward."

This shift in perspective can lead to a more grounded and peaceful life. When you can observe your thoughts and emotions without judgment, you reduce the power they have over you. You become less reactive and more responsive, able to make choices that align with your values and goals. This resilience is particularly crucial in the face of future challenges. Instead of being overwhelmed by new difficulties, you have the tools to approach them with a calm and clear mind.

Moreover, cultivating the observing self can enhance your relationships. When you are less reactive to your own emotions, you can be more present and empathetic with others. You can listen more deeply, understand their perspectives, and respond with compassion. This can lead to stronger, more fulfilling connections, which in turn provide a supportive network that further bolsters your emotional well-being.

In essence, the long-term benefits of cultivating the observing self are profound. It empowers you to live a life that is not dictated by past traumas but is instead guided by your values and aspirations. You can navigate the ups and downs of life with a sense of balance and purpose, knowing that you have the inner strength to face whatever comes your way. This perspective is not just a coping mechanism; it is a way of life that can lead to greater peace, resilience, and fulfillment.

Chapter Eight

Rediscovering What Truly Matters

"Your values are the compass that guides your life. They are the non-negotiable principles that give your actions purpose and your life meaning."

In the aftermath of trauma, the world can often feel like a place devoid of direction and purpose. The once-clear paths that guided our lives may seem obscured by the fog of painful memories and emotions. Yet, it is in these moments of darkness that the importance of values becomes most apparent. Values are the lighthouses that illuminate our way forward, helping us to rediscover what truly matters and to chart a course toward a more fulfilling and meaningful life.

Acceptance and Commitment Therapy (ACT) places a significant emphasis on values. In the context of trauma recovery, values serve as the foundation upon which we can rebuild our lives. They are the bedrock that supports us as we navigate the challenging terrain of healing and growth. When we clarify our values, we gain a sense of purpose and direction that can be profoundly empowering. This process is not about erasing the past or ignoring our pain; it is about acknowledging our experiences and choosing to move forward in a way that aligns with what we hold dear.

Imagine, for a moment, a person who has survived a traumatic event. The initial shock and distress can make it difficult to see beyond the immediate pain. However, as they begin to engage in values clarification, they start to reconnect with their core beliefs and aspirations. They might realize that family, creativity, or helping others are values that still hold deep meaning for them. This realization can be a powerful catalyst for change. It can transform the way they view their trauma, shifting the focus from what they have lost to what they can still gain.

Values clarification is a dynamic process that involves introspection, self-discovery, and sometimes, redefining what matters most. It is not a one-time event but a journey that unfolds over time. As we explore our values, we may find that some have remained constant, while others have evolved in response to our experiences. This process of rediscovery can be deeply healing, as it allows us to integrate our past with our present and future.

In trauma recovery, values provide a framework for making decisions and setting goals. When we know what truly matters to us, we can make choices that align with our deeper aspirations. This alignment can bring a sense of coherence and purpose to our lives, even in the face of adversity. For example, if someone values resilience, they might choose to engage in activities that build their inner strength and coping skills. If they value connection, they might prioritize rebuilding relationships and seeking support from loved ones.

Moreover, values can serve as a source of motivation and resilience. When we are clear about what we stand for, we are better equipped to face challenges and overcome obstacles. This clarity can help us stay committed to our recovery journey, even when the path ahead seems daunting. It can also provide a sense of fulfillment and satisfaction, as we see our actions and efforts align with our deepest values.

In the following pages, we will delve deeper into the process of values clarification. We will explore practical exercises and strategies that can help you identify and live in accordance with your values. This chapter is designed to be a supportive and encouraging guide, offering you the tools and insights you need to rediscover what truly matters and to move forward with confidence and purpose.

Remember, your values are unique to you, and they are the compass that will guide you on your journey to healing and a more fulfilling life. As you embark on this process, be gentle with yourself and open to the possibilities that lie ahead. Your values are waiting to be rediscovered, and they have the power to transform your life in ways you may not yet imagine.

The Role of Values in Trauma Recovery

Reconnecting with personal values is a powerful and transformative process for trauma survivors, one that can significantly aid in moving forward and building a meaningful life. Trauma has a way of fracturing the very core of who we are, often leaving us feeling lost, disconnected, and adrift in a sea of painful memories and emotions. It can erode our sense of purpose and identity, making it difficult to see a path forward. In the aftermath of trauma, many individuals find themselves disconnected from the things that once gave their lives meaning and direction. This disconnection can manifest in various ways—loss of interest in activities once enjoyed, a sense of numbness or detachment, or a pervasive feeling of emptiness. The process of values clarification, however, offers a beacon of hope, a way to navigate through the fog of trauma and rediscover the essence of what truly matters.

When we experience trauma, it is not uncommon for our core values to become obscured or overshadowed by the overwhelming nature of our experiences. Trauma can create a lens through which we view the world that is clouded by fear, pain, and a sense of helplessness. This lens can distort our perception of what is important, leading us to prioritize survival and avoidance over growth and fulfillment. However, by engaging in the process of values clarification, we can begin to peel back these layers and uncover the values that have always been there, waiting to be rediscovered.

Values are the guiding principles that give our lives direction and purpose. They are the internal compass that helps us navigate the world, making decisions and taking actions that align with who we are and what we stand for. For trauma survivors, reconnecting with these values can be a profound act of self-compassion and self-care. It allows us to reconnect with the parts of ourselves that may have been buried or forgotten, and it provides a framework for rebuilding our lives in a way that is authentic and meaningful.

In this chapter, we will explore various techniques and exercises designed to help you rediscover your core values. These exercises are not just about identifying what matters to you; they are about deeply understanding and integrating these values into your daily life. We will delve into the ways in which trauma can distort our values and how to recognize and challenge these distortions. By doing so, you will be better equipped to make choices that align with your true self, rather than being driven by the remnants of trauma.

The process of values clarification is not just about looking inward; it is also about looking outward and seeing the world through a new, more hopeful lens. When we reconnect with our values, we gain a sense of clarity and direction that can be incredibly empowering. It allows us to set goals and take actions that are in line with our deepest desires and aspirations, rather than being dictated by the fear and pain of the past. This shift in perspective can be transformative, helping us to build a life that is not only free from the constraints of trauma but also rich with meaning and purpose.

As you embark on this journey of values clarification, remember that it is a process of rediscovery and growth. It is about reconnecting with the parts of yourself that have always been there, even in the darkest moments. By embracing this process, you can begin to build a life that is not just about surviving but about thriving. You can reclaim your power, find your voice, and live a life that is true to who you are and what you value most. This chapter is your guide to that journey, offering you the tools and support you need to rediscover what truly matters and to live a life that reflects your deepest values and aspirations.

Identifying Your Core Values

Values are the guiding lights that steer us through life, helping us make decisions and find meaning even in the darkest moments. When we have experienced trauma, these values can become obscured, making it all the more important to uncover and reconnect with them. Here, we will explore a gentle and introspective process to help you identify and clarify your core values.

Begin by finding a quiet, comfortable space where you can sit and reflect without interruption. Close your eyes and take a few deep breaths, allowing yourself to settle into the present moment. As you breathe in, imagine drawing in a sense of peace and calm. As you exhale, release any tension or distractions. This simple act of breathing can help you center yourself and prepare for the deeper work ahead.

Now, think about a time in your life when you felt truly alive, when you were fully engaged and connected to something meaningful. It could be a moment of joy, a significant achievement, or a time when you felt a deep sense of purpose. What was happening in that moment? What were you doing, and how did you feel? Allow the memory to unfold in your mind, and pay attention to the emotions and sensations that arise. What values do you think were being honored in that moment? Was it a sense of connection, creativity, or perhaps a feeling of making a difference?

Next, consider the people in your life who you admire and respect. What qualities do they possess that you find inspiring? What about their actions or way of being resonates with you? These qualities can often be a reflection of your own values. For example, if you admire someone for their kindness and empathy, it's likely that these are values that are important to you as well. Reflect on why these qualities stand out to you and how they might align with your own sense of what matters most.

Now, imagine a future version of yourself, living a life that is deeply fulfilling and aligned with your core values. What does this life look like? What are you doing, and who are you with? What kind of impact are you making on the world around you? Visualize this future with as much detail as possible, and notice the values that emerge. Are you living a life of service, creativity, or perhaps one of adventure and exploration? Each of these visions can provide clues about what truly matters to you.

As you reflect on these questions, it can be helpful to write down your thoughts and insights. Journaling can be a powerful tool for self-discovery, allowing you to explore your feelings and ideas in a more structured way. You might find it useful to create a list of potential values that come to mind, such as love, integrity, growth, or freedom. Take your time with this list, adding to it as new values emerge and refining it as you gain clarity.

Once you have a list of potential values, consider which ones resonate the most deeply. You can do this by asking yourself, "If I had to choose, which of these values would I prioritize in my life?" This process of prioritization can help you narrow down your list to the core values that truly define who you are and what you stand for. It's important to remember that there is no right or wrong number of core values. Some people may have just a few, while others may have more. The key is to identify the values that feel most authentic and meaningful to you.

As you continue to explore your values, be gentle with yourself. This is a process of discovery, and it may take time to fully uncover what truly matters to you. It's okay to revisit and refine your values as you grow and change. The important thing is to stay open and curious, allowing yourself to be guided by your inner wisdom.

In the context of trauma-focused ACT, values clarification is not just about identifying what matters most; it's also about committing to living in alignment with these values, even in the face of challenging thoughts and emotions. By reconnecting with your core values, you can find a sense of direction and purpose that can help you navigate the path of healing and transformation. As you move forward, remember that each step you take toward living a values-driven life is a step toward reclaiming your power and regaining control of your life.

Aligning Your Actions with Your Values

Aligning one's daily actions with their values is a cornerstone of emotional resilience and a profound source of fulfillment. When we live in accordance with what truly matters to us, we create a sense of coherence and purpose that can buffer us against the challenges of life, especially those that stem from traumatic experiences. Values are the guiding stars that direct our path, and by actively choosing to follow them, we can transform our lives into a meaningful journey rather than a series of disjointed events.

Consider the metaphor of a ship navigating through stormy seas. The ship's compass, which points to its true north, is akin to our values. Without a clear direction, the ship is at the mercy of the wind and waves, just as we can feel adrift and overwhelmed without a sense of purpose. However, when we have a clear compass and a steadfast captain, the ship can weather the storm and reach its destination. Similarly, when we align our actions with our values, we can face life's challenges with greater strength and resilience.

One practical strategy for making values-based decisions in everyday life is to start with a values clarification exercise. Take some quiet time to reflect on what truly matters to you. What are the principles and qualities that you hold dear? Is it family, creativity, integrity, or community service? Write these values down and keep them in a visible place, such as on a note on your fridge or as a screensaver on your phone. This constant reminder can serve as a gentle nudge to make choices that align with your core values.

Another effective approach is to practice mindfulness. By cultivating a present-moment awareness, you can become more attuned to your values and the choices that honor them. For example, if one of your values is compassion, you might find that being more mindful helps you notice opportunities to show kindness to others, even in small ways. This could be as simple as listening attentively to a friend or offering a word of encouragement to a colleague. Each small act of compassion reinforces your value and deepens your sense of fulfillment.

Setting clear intentions at the start of each day can also help you stay aligned with your values. In the morning, take a few minutes to reflect on what you want to achieve and how you can live in accordance with your values. You might write down a few key intentions, such as being patient with your partner, focusing on your health, or contributing to a project that matters to you. Throughout the day, check in with yourself to see if your actions are aligned with these intentions. If you find that you've strayed, gently redirect yourself back to your values.

Creating a values-based action plan can provide a structured way to integrate your values into your daily life. Identify specific actions you can take each week to live in alignment with your values. For instance, if your value is health, you might commit to going for a daily walk or preparing healthy meals. If your value is learning, you might set aside time each week to read a book or take an online course. By breaking down your values into actionable steps, you make it easier to stay on track and see tangible progress.

Lastly, it's important to celebrate your successes, no matter how small. Each time you make a values-based decision, take a moment to acknowledge and appreciate yourself. This positive reinforcement can build your confidence and motivation to continue living in alignment with your values. Remember, the journey of values-based living is not about perfection but about progress. By consistently choosing actions that reflect what truly matters to you, you can foster emotional resilience and a deep sense of fulfillment, ultimately regaining control of your life and creating a meaningful path forward.

Overcoming Barriers to Living a Values-Based Life

Living in alignment with your values after experiencing trauma can feel like an uphill battle. The emotional and psychological scars left by traumatic events can create significant barriers that make it difficult to move forward. One of the most common barriers is fear. Fear can manifest in many ways, from the fear of re-experiencing the trauma to the fear of the unknown. This fear can paralyze you, making it challenging to take the steps necessary to live a life that aligns with your values. For example, if you value creativity and want to pursue a career in the arts, the fear of failure or judgment might hold you back. To overcome this, it's essential to acknowledge and accept your fear without judgment. Recognize that fear is a natural part of the healing process and that it doesn't define you. Start by setting small, achievable goals that align with your values. For instance, if you want to become a writer, begin by journaling for a few minutes each day. Gradually increase the time and complexity of your writing as you build confidence and resilience.

Self-doubt is another significant barrier that trauma survivors often face. Trauma can erode your sense of self-worth and make it difficult to trust your own decisions and abilities. This self-doubt can lead to a cycle of negative self-talk and self-sabotage. To combat self-doubt, it's crucial to cultivate self-compassion. Treat yourself with the same kindness and understanding you would offer to a close friend. When negative thoughts arise, acknowledge them but don't dwell on them. Instead, focus on your strengths and the progress you've made. Keep a journal of your accomplishments, no matter how small, and refer to it when self-doubt creeps in. Additionally, seek out supportive relationships with people who believe in you and your abilities. Their encouragement can provide the boost you need to keep moving forward.

External pressures can also pose significant challenges. Family, friends, and societal expectations can sometimes push you in directions that don't align with your values. For example, if your family expects you to pursue a traditional career path, but your heart lies in social work, you might feel torn and conflicted. It's important to set boundaries and communicate your needs clearly. Let those around you know what is important to you and why. When you assert your values, you empower yourself to make choices that are true to who you are. Surround yourself with people who respect your boundaries and support your goals. If necessary, seek the help of a therapist or counselor who can provide guidance and strategies for navigating these pressures.

Another barrier is the tendency to avoid situations that trigger painful memories or emotions. While avoidance can provide temporary relief, it can also prevent you from fully engaging in life and living in alignment with your values. To overcome this, practice mindfulness and grounding techniques. When you encounter a trigger, take a moment to breathe deeply and focus on the present moment. Notice the sensations in your body, the sounds around you, and the sensations of the ground beneath your feet. This can help you stay centered and reduce the intensity of the trigger. Gradually expose yourself to situations that you have been avoiding, starting with less challenging ones and working your way up. Each small step you take is a victory and brings you closer to living a life that is true to your values.

Lastly, the feeling of being stuck or overwhelmed can be a significant barrier. Trauma can leave you feeling like you're trapped in a cycle of pain and struggle. To break free from this, it's important to break down your goals into manageable steps. Instead of focusing on the end result, focus on the process and the small actions you can take each day. Celebrate each milestone, no matter how small, and use these victories to build momentum. Remember that healing and growth are not linear processes. There will be setbacks and challenges, but each step you take, no matter how small, is a step toward a more fulfilling and meaningful life. By addressing these barriers with understanding and actionable strategies, you can move closer to living a life that is true to your values and aligned with your deepest desires.

The Long-Term Benefits of Values-Based Living

Living in accordance with one's values is a profound and transformative practice that can significantly enhance emotional stability, fulfillment, and a sense of purpose. When we align our daily actions and decisions with our core values, we create a life that feels authentic and meaningful. This alignment is not just a fleeting feeling of satisfaction; it is a long-term investment in our well-being that pays dividends in many aspects of our lives.

Consider the example of Emily, a trauma survivor who values resilience and community. After a series of traumatic events, Emily found herself struggling to regain a sense of control and purpose. She began to explore how she could live her values more fully. Emily started by volunteering at a local support group for trauma survivors, where she could both receive and offer support. This act of giving back not only helped her feel more connected to others but also reinforced her own resilience. Over time, Emily noticed that her emotional stability improved. She felt less overwhelmed by her past and more capable of handling life's challenges. Her involvement in the community also provided a sense of belonging, which is crucial for emotional well-being.

Another example is John, who values creativity and innovation. After a traumatic experience, John felt stuck and unable to tap into his creative side. He decided to take a class in digital art, something he had always been interested in but never pursued. By dedicating time to this activity, John began to rediscover his passion for creating. This not only brought joy and fulfillment into his life but also helped him process his trauma in a new and constructive way. The act of creating allowed him to express his emotions and experiences in a safe and therapeutic manner. John's renewed sense of purpose and creativity became a powerful force in his recovery, giving him a renewed sense of direction and hope.

Living in accordance with one's values also fosters a deeper sense of fulfillment. When we engage in activities that align with what we hold dear, we experience a profound sense of satisfaction. This fulfillment is not just about achieving goals; it is about the ongoing process of living a life that feels true to who we are. For instance, Sarah, who values personal growth and learning, made a commitment to read a new book every month. This practice not only expanded her knowledge but also provided her with a sense of continuous growth and self-improvement. Each book she read offered new insights and perspectives, enriching her life in ways she had not anticipated. Sarah's commitment to learning became a cornerstone of her well-being, providing her with a sense of purpose and direction.

Moreover, values-based living can enhance our relationships and social connections. When we live in a way that reflects our values, we attract people who share similar beliefs and interests. This can lead to deeper and more meaningful connections. For example, Alex, who values authenticity and honesty, made a conscious effort to be more open and genuine in his interactions with others. This shift in his approach to relationships led to more meaningful conversations and a stronger sense of trust with his friends and family. Alex found that his relationships became more fulfilling and supportive, which in turn contributed to his overall well-being.

In the long term, living in accordance with our values can also protect us from the negative effects of stress and trauma. When we have a clear sense of what is important to us, we are better equipped to navigate life's challenges. This clarity helps us make decisions that are aligned with our well-being, rather than being swayed by external pressures or short-term gains. For instance, Lisa, who values health and well-being, made a commitment to prioritize self-care and physical activity. This commitment not only improved her physical health but also provided her with a sense of control and resilience in the face of adversity. Lisa's values-based approach to health became a buffer against the stressors of daily life, helping her maintain her emotional stability and overall well-being.

In essence, living in accordance with our values is a powerful way to build a life that is both fulfilling and meaningful. It provides a foundation for emotional stability, a sense of purpose, and a deeper connection to the world around us. By aligning our actions with our core values, we create a life that feels authentic and purposeful, one that is resilient and full of hope.

Chapter 9

Committed Action – Moving Forward with Purpose

"Action may not always bring happiness, but there is no happiness without action."
Benjamin Disraeli

The weight of painful memories and emotions can feel like an insurmountable barrier, making it difficult to envision a future where you are in control of your life. However, the concept of committed action in Acceptance and Commitment Therapy (ACT) offers a powerful framework for breaking through these barriers and moving forward with purpose. Committed action is about taking meaningful steps, aligned with your values, to create a life that is rich, full, and meaningful, despite the presence of pain.

When we talk about committed action, we are not referring to the kind of action that is driven by avoidance or fear. Instead, it is about making a conscious choice to engage in behaviors that align with what truly matters to you. This might mean taking small steps to reconnect with loved ones, pursuing a long-abandoned hobby, or even making a career change that aligns with your values. The key is to act in a way that is congruent with your deepest aspirations, even when it feels challenging.

For individuals who have experienced trauma, the concept of committed action can be particularly transformative. Trauma often leaves a legacy of disconnection and a sense of helplessness. It can feel as though the past has a stranglehold on the present, making it hard to envision a future that is different from the one you have known. However, by focusing on values-based actions, you can begin to reclaim a sense of control and direction in your life. Each step you take, no matter how small, is a step towards a life that is more aligned with who you are and what you want to achieve.

One of the most compelling aspects of committed action is its ability to foster a sense of empowerment. When you take action that is meaningful to you, you are not just passively enduring your circumstances; you are actively shaping your life. This shift from passivity to agency is crucial in trauma recovery. It allows you to move from a place of victimhood to a place of strength and resilience. By consistently taking values-based actions, you build a foundation of self-efficacy and confidence, which are essential for long-term healing and growth.

Moreover, committed action helps to break the cycle of rumination and avoidance that often accompanies trauma. When you are actively engaged in pursuing your values, you are less likely to get caught up in the painful thoughts and emotions that can dominate your mind.

Instead, you are focused on the present moment and the actions you are taking to create a better future. This shift in focus can be incredibly liberating, as it allows you to live more fully in the present and to experience a greater sense of joy and fulfillment.

It's important to recognize that committed action is not about perfection or achieving some idealized version of yourself. It's about making consistent, values-based choices that move you in the direction of a more meaningful life. This might mean making mistakes, facing setbacks, and experiencing moments of doubt. But each step, no matter how small, is a step towards a life that is more aligned with your true self.

What Is Committed Action?

In the realm of Trauma-Focused Acceptance and Commitment Therapy (TF-ACT), committed action is a powerful and transformative principle that involves taking intentional steps aligned with one's deeply held values. It is not just about doing things but doing them with purpose and meaning. Committed action means making a conscious decision to engage in behaviors that move you closer to the life you truly want to live, despite the presence of painful thoughts and emotions. It is about bridging the gap between where you are now and where you aspire to be, by consistently taking actions that reflect your core values.

Imagine you have a compass, and your values are the magnetic north that guides your journey. Committed action is the steady, intentional movement toward that north, even when the terrain is rough and the weather is stormy. It's about making choices that honor your deepest desires and commitments, even when it feels challenging or scary. For example, if one of your values is connection, committed action might involve reaching out to a friend or family member, even if you feel anxious or isolated. If your value is growth, it might mean taking a small step toward a new skill or goal, even if you feel uncertain or afraid of failure.

The beauty of committed action lies in its emphasis on the process rather than the outcome. It's about the journey and the effort, not just the destination. Small actions, when taken consistently, can create significant and lasting change. Think of it like planting a garden. Each seed you plant is a small action, but over time, with consistent effort and care, those seeds grow into a beautiful and thriving garden. Similarly, each small step you take toward your values, no matter how minor it may seem, can lead to profound transformations in your life.

Committed action is also about flexibility and resilience. It's not about being perfect or never feeling pain; it's about continuing to move forward despite the obstacles. If you encounter a roadblock, you find another path. If you fall, you get back up. This resilience is what builds your psychological flexibility, allowing you to navigate life's challenges with greater ease and purpose. By aligning your actions with your values, you create a life that is not only meaningful but also deeply satisfying. You are no longer a passive observer of your life; you are an active participant, shaping your world with intention and courage.

Setting Goals for Trauma Recovery

Setting realistic, values-based goals for your trauma recovery journey is a crucial step in regaining control over your life. It's about aligning your actions with what truly matters to you, and it's a process that requires both intention and compassion. When you set goals that are deeply rooted in your values, you create a roadmap that not only guides you but also gives you a sense of purpose and direction. This chapter will help you navigate this process, offering practical tips and supportive guidance to ensure your goals are both meaningful and achievable.

First, take some time to reflect on your values. What are the things that matter most to you? Are they related to your relationships, personal growth, career, or perhaps community involvement? Values are the core principles that give your life meaning and direction. They are not the same as goals, which are specific and measurable, but they are the foundation upon which your goals are built. For example, if one of your values is family, a goal might be to spend more quality time with your loved ones. If your value is personal growth, a goal could be to take a course or read books that challenge and expand your knowledge.

Once you have a clear understanding of your values, it's time to set specific goals. It's important to make these goals realistic and attainable. Setting overly ambitious goals can lead to frustration and a sense of failure, which can be particularly detrimental when you are in the process of healing from trauma. Instead, aim for goals that are challenging yet achievable. For instance, if your value is health and well-being, a realistic goal might be to go for a 10-minute walk every day, rather than committing to an hour-long workout that you might struggle to maintain.

Breaking down large goals into smaller, manageable steps is a powerful strategy for ensuring success. This approach, known as "chunking," helps to make the process less overwhelming and more actionable. For example, if your goal is to write a book, you might start by setting a goal to write one page a day. This small, consistent effort can lead to significant progress over time. Similarly, if your goal is to improve your relationships, you might start by setting aside 15 minutes each day to connect with a loved one through a phone call or a text message. These small actions can build into a habit that strengthens your relationships over time.

Another important aspect of setting and achieving goals is to be flexible and kind to yourself. Trauma recovery is a nonlinear process, and there will be times when you face setbacks or feel stuck. When this happens, it's essential to recognize that these are normal parts of the journey. Instead of giving up, take a moment to reassess your goals and adjust them if necessary. Perhaps you need to take a break, seek additional support, or modify your approach. The key is to stay committed to your values and to keep moving forward, even if it's at a slower pace.

It can also be helpful to create a support system that can help you stay accountable and motivated. This might include friends, family members, a therapist, or a support group. Share your goals with them and ask for their encouragement and support. Knowing that you have people who believe in you and are there to help can make a significant difference in your ability to stay on track.

Lastly, celebrate your progress, no matter how small. Recognize and acknowledge the effort you are putting in and the steps you are taking toward your goals. This can boost your motivation and help you stay positive. Whether it's treating yourself to a favorite meal, taking a relaxing bath, or simply taking a moment to feel proud of yourself, these celebrations are important for maintaining your momentum and reinforcing the idea that you are capable of achieving your goals.

By setting realistic, values-based goals and breaking them down into manageable steps, you can create a path forward that is both purposeful and achievable. This process is not just about reaching a destination; it's about the journey of growth and healing that you are undertaking. With each step, you are moving closer to a life that is aligned with your deepest values and aspirations.

Overcoming Obstacles to Taking Action

One of the most common barriers is the fear of failure. This fear can be deeply rooted in past experiences where attempts to change or improve were met with setbacks or even further trauma. The weight of this fear can paralyze even the most determined individuals, making it seem safer to stay in a familiar, albeit painful, state rather than risk another disappointment. However, it's important to remember that failure is not the end but a step in the process of growth. Each attempt, whether successful or not, provides valuable lessons and builds resilience. To overcome this fear, it can be helpful to reframe failure as a learning opportunity. Instead of viewing setbacks as a reflection of your worth, see them as chances to gain insights and refine your approach. Celebrate small victories along the way, no matter how minor they may seem, to build confidence and momentum.

Procrastination is another significant obstacle that can hinder progress. It's easy to get caught in a cycle of putting things off, often rationalizing that the timing isn't right or that you need more information before taking action. Trauma can exacerbate this tendency, as the overwhelming nature of the task can feel insurmountable. To combat procrastination, break down your goals into manageable steps. Start with small, achievable tasks that feel less daunting. For example, if your goal is to start a new job, begin by updating your resume or reaching out to a mentor for advice. By taking small, consistent actions, you build a sense of accomplishment and reduce the feeling of being overwhelmed. Additionally, setting specific deadlines and holding yourself accountable can provide the structure needed to stay on track.

Self-doubt is a pervasive issue that can erode confidence and make it difficult to take committed action. Trauma can leave deep scars on your self-esteem, making it easy to second-guess your abilities and decisions. It's important to recognize that self-doubt is a natural part of the process and that everyone, regardless of their past, experiences moments of uncertainty. To combat self-doubt, practice self-compassion. Treat yourself with the same kindness and understanding you would offer to a friend. Challenge negative self-talk by reframing critical thoughts into more supportive and realistic ones. For instance, instead of thinking, "I can't do this," try, "I can take one small step at a time." Surrounding yourself with a supportive network of friends, family, or a therapist can also provide the encouragement and validation you need to keep moving forward.

Another common obstacle is the fear of reliving trauma. The thought of confronting painful memories or situations can be so overwhelming that it feels safer to avoid them altogether. However, avoidance can become a barrier to healing and growth. To address this, it's crucial to approach these challenges with a sense of curiosity and openness. Mindfulness practices, such as deep breathing or grounding techniques, can help you stay present and manage the intensity of emotions. Gradual exposure, under the guidance of a therapist, can also be a powerful tool. By slowly and safely confronting your fears, you build the resilience and coping skills needed to navigate them more effectively.

Finally, maintaining consistency is key to overcoming these obstacles. It's easy to start strong but lose steam over time. To stay consistent, set realistic goals and create a routine that supports your progress. Regularly reflect on your values and the reasons why you are taking committed action. This can help you stay motivated and aligned with your deeper purpose. Celebrate your progress, no matter how small, and be gentle with yourself when setbacks occur. Remember, the journey of healing and growth is not linear, and each step forward, no matter how small, is a step toward a more fulfilling and meaningful life.

Building Resilience Through Committed Action

Taking committed action is a powerful tool for building emotional resilience and helping trauma survivors regain control over their lives. When you align your actions with your core values, you create a sense of purpose and direction that can transform even the most challenging moments into opportunities for growth. This is not about ignoring the pain or the trauma; it's about acknowledging it and choosing to move forward despite it.

Imagine a person who has experienced a significant trauma, such as a car accident that left them with physical and emotional scars. Initially, the pain and fear might be overwhelming, making it difficult to envision a future where they can live a fulfilling life. However, by taking small, consistent actions that align with their values, they can gradually rebuild their sense of control and purpose. For example, if one of their core values is family, they might start by spending more quality time with their loved ones, even if it feels challenging at first. This might involve simple activities like sharing a meal together or going for a walk. Over time, these actions can become a source of strength and comfort, reinforcing the idea that they are more than their trauma.

Committed action is not just about the big, dramatic steps; it's about the daily choices that add up to significant change. For instance, someone who values personal growth might decide to start a journal to process their thoughts and emotions. Each entry is a small step, but collectively, they can lead to profound insights and healing. As they write, they might notice patterns in their thinking or identify areas where they need additional support. This process of self-reflection and intentional action is a powerful way to build emotional resilience. It teaches them that they have the capacity to manage their emotions and make choices that align with their values, even in the face of adversity.

Another example is a person who values creativity and finds solace in art. They might start by dedicating a few minutes each day to drawing or painting. At first, it might feel like a struggle, but as they continue to commit to this practice, they will likely find that it becomes a source of joy and healing. The act of creating something beautiful can be a powerful antidote to the feelings of helplessness and despair that often accompany trauma. It allows them to express their emotions in a tangible way and to see that they are capable of producing something positive and meaningful.

Moreover, committed action helps trauma survivors reclaim their sense of agency. When you take consistent, values-based actions, you are actively choosing to live the life you want, rather than being passively shaped by your past. This sense of control is crucial for healing and personal growth. For example, someone who values community might volunteer at a local shelter or join a support group. These actions not only help others but also provide a sense of purpose and connection. They remind the individual that they have a role to play in the world and that their actions can make a difference.

Committed action is a powerful tool for emotional resilience because it helps trauma survivors reconnect with their values and live a life that is meaningful and fulfilling. It is about taking small, consistent steps that align with who you are and what you believe in. Each action, no matter how small, is a step towards reclaiming your life and building a future that is filled with hope and possibility. By choosing to move forward with purpose, you are not only healing yourself but also inspiring others to do the same.

Creating a Roadmap for Long-Term Action

Creating a long-term roadmap for committed action is a crucial step in your journey toward healing and living a meaningful life after trauma. It's about setting a course that aligns with your values and aspirations, and it involves both short-term and long-term goals. The process can be both practical and inspiring, helping you to see the path forward with clarity and purpose.

To begin, it's essential to reflect on what truly matters to you. What are the values that you hold dear, and how do you want to live your life? These values will serve as the North Star, guiding your actions and decisions. Once you have a clear understanding of your values, you can start setting specific goals that are aligned with them. For instance, if one of your values is to nurture meaningful relationships, a short-term goal might be to schedule a weekly phone call with a close friend, while a long-term goal could be to organize a reunion with old friends or join a social group that shares your interests.

Setting short-term goals is vital because they provide immediate direction and a sense of accomplishment. These goals should be achievable within a relatively short period, such as a few weeks or months. They serve as stepping stones that build momentum and confidence. For example, if you value personal growth, a short-term goal might be to read one book on a topic that interests you each month. This not only helps you stay engaged and motivated but also lays the foundation for more significant achievements.

Long-term goals, on the other hand, are the big picture aspirations that you want to achieve over several years. They require more planning and commitment, but they are what drive your overall progress. A long-term goal might be to complete a degree, start a business, or write a book. To make these goals more manageable, break them down into smaller, intermediate steps. For instance, if your long-term goal is to write a book, your intermediate steps might include outlining the chapters, setting a daily writing schedule, and finding a writing group for support and feedback.

Tracking your progress is essential for maintaining motivation and making adjustments as needed. One effective way to do this is by keeping a journal or a progress log. Write down your goals, the steps you are taking, and any challenges you encounter. Reflect on what is working and what isn't, and be honest with yourself about any setbacks. This reflection will help you stay accountable and make informed decisions about your next steps. For example, if you find that you are consistently struggling to meet a particular goal, it might be time to reassess and adjust your approach. Perhaps you need to break it down into even smaller steps or seek additional support.

Flexibility is key in committed action. Life is unpredictable, and it's natural for your goals and circumstances to change over time. Be open to adjusting your plans as needed. This doesn't mean giving up on your values or long-term aspirations, but rather finding new ways to pursue them. For instance, if a personal or professional crisis arises, you might need to temporarily shift your focus to address immediate needs. Once the crisis is managed, you can return to your original goals with renewed energy and perspective.

Another important aspect of committed action is finding sources of support. No one achieves their goals in isolation, and having a support system can make a significant difference. This might include friends, family, therapists, mentors, or support groups. Share your goals with people who can offer encouragement, provide feedback, and help you stay on track. Their belief in you can be a powerful motivator, especially during challenging times.

Lastly, celebrate your successes, no matter how small they may seem. Each step forward, no matter how incremental, is a victory. Recognize and acknowledge your progress, and allow yourself to feel proud of what you have accomplished. This positive reinforcement will fuel your motivation and reinforce your commitment to your goals.

By creating a long-term roadmap for committed action, you are taking a proactive and purposeful approach to your life. This journey is about more than just achieving goals; it's about living a life that is aligned with your values and finding fulfillment in the process. With each step, you are moving closer to the life you want to live, one filled with meaning, purpose, and resilience.

Chapter 10

The Path Forward – Integrating Trauma-Focused ACT into Daily Life

"Trauma is not just an event that happened to us. It is the residue of that experience that gets left behind in our minds and bodies."
Peter A. Levine, Ph.D.

As we reach the final chapter of this journey, it is important to take a moment to reflect on the path we have traveled together. From the initial steps of understanding trauma and its impact on our lives, to the foundational principles of Acceptance and Commitment Therapy (ACT), we have explored a myriad of tools and strategies to help navigate the complex emotions and thoughts that trauma can bring. Now, as we stand at the threshold of a new beginning, it is time to consider how we can integrate these principles into our daily lives to foster sustained healing and growth.

Throughout this book, we have delved into the essence of psychological flexibility—learning to accept what we cannot control while committing to actions that align with our values. We have uncovered the power of mindfulness, the importance of values, and the role of defusion in managing painful thoughts and memories. Each of these principles is not just a theoretical concept but a practical tool that can be woven into the fabric of our everyday existence.

Integrating Trauma-Focused ACT into daily life is about more than just applying techniques; it is about cultivating a mindset that supports ongoing healing and growth. It is about recognizing that healing is not a destination but a continuous journey. Each day presents new opportunities to practice acceptance, to engage in meaningful activities, and to reconnect with the parts of ourselves that trauma may have pushed aside.

Consider the morning routine. Instead of starting the day with a rush of anxiety and stress, you can begin with a few moments of mindfulness. Take a deep breath, feel the air fill your lungs, and let the tension in your body release with each exhale. This simple act can set a tone of calm and presence, allowing you to approach the day with a clearer mind and a more centered heart.

Throughout the day, you can use defusion techniques to manage intrusive thoughts and memories. When a painful memory arises, instead of pushing it away, try to observe it as if it were a passing cloud in the sky. Acknowledge its presence without letting it dictate your actions. This can help you stay grounded in the present moment, even when the past feels heavy.

In the evenings, reflect on the values that guide your life. What actions did you take today that aligned with these values? What can you do differently tomorrow to move closer to them? This practice of values-based living can transform your life in profound ways, bringing a sense of purpose and fulfillment that trauma may have obscured.

Integrating these principles is also about building a supportive community. Reach out to friends, family, or a therapist who understand your journey. Share your experiences, your struggles, and your triumphs. This connection can provide a sense of belonging and reduce the isolation that trauma can often bring.

Remember, healing is not a linear process. There will be setbacks and challenges, but each step forward, no matter how small, is a step toward a more meaningful and fulfilling life. By integrating Trauma-Focused ACT into your daily life, you are not just managing the symptoms of trauma; you are actively creating a life that is rich with meaning and purpose.

As you move forward, carry these lessons with you. Embrace the challenges with courage and the victories with gratitude. You have the tools and the strength to build the life you desire. The journey continues, and with each step, you are regaining control and finding a path to healing and growth.

Applying ACT Principles in Everyday Situations

These principles, including cognitive defusion, emotional expansion, and committed action, are powerful tools that can help you manage painful thoughts and experiences while moving toward a more fulfilling life.

Imagine waking up one morning, feeling the weight of a traumatic memory pressing down on you. Instead of trying to push it away or ignore it, you can practice cognitive defusion. This involves stepping back from your thoughts and seeing them for what they are—just words and images, not facts. For example, if you find yourself thinking, "I'm broken and will never recover," you can gently remind yourself, "I'm having the thought that I'm broken and will never recover." This simple shift in perspective can create a bit of distance, allowing you to observe the thought without getting entangled in it. As you go about your morning routine, you can continue to practice this by noticing other thoughts and labeling them as just thoughts. This practice can be done while brushing your teeth, making coffee, or even during a short walk.

Emotional expansion is another crucial principle that can be woven into your daily life. This involves making room for difficult emotions without judgment. When you feel a wave of sadness or anxiety, instead of fighting it, you can acknowledge it and allow it to be there. For instance, if you're sitting in traffic and feel a surge of frustration, you might say to yourself, "I'm feeling frustrated right now, and that's okay." You can then take a few deep breaths and focus on the physical sensations in your body, such as the rise and fall of your chest or the feeling of your feet on the floor. This practice helps you develop a greater capacity to tolerate uncomfortable emotions, making them less overwhelming and more manageable.

Committed action is about taking steps toward your values, even when it's difficult. This can be as simple as setting a small, achievable goal each day that aligns with what matters most to you. For example, if one of your values is connection, you might decide to call a friend or family member for a quick chat during your lunch break. If your value is health, you could commit to taking a 10-minute walk after dinner. These small actions, when done consistently, can add up to significant changes over time. By focusing on what you can do today, you're taking control of your life and moving in a direction that feels meaningful.

In the context of daily routines, you can also incorporate mindfulness exercises to enhance your overall well-being. For instance, while you're washing dishes, you can focus on the sensation of the warm water on your hands, the smell of the dish soap, and the sound of the water running. This simple act of being present can help you stay grounded and reduce the grip of painful thoughts and emotions. Similarly, when you're walking your dog, you can pay attention to the feel of the leash in your hand, the sounds of nature around you, and the warmth of the sun on your skin. These moments of mindfulness can be brief but powerful, helping you stay connected to the present moment and reducing the intensity of traumatic memories.

Another practical way to integrate these principles is by using values cards or a values journal. You can create a list of your core values and keep it somewhere visible, like on your refrigerator or as a screensaver on your phone. Each morning, take a moment to reflect on one or two values and consider how you can bring them to life that day. For example, if one of your values is growth, you might decide to read a few pages of a self-help book or try a new hobby. This practice helps you stay aligned with what truly matters to you, even on the toughest days.

By incorporating these principles into your daily life, you can build a stronger foundation of psychological flexibility. Each small step you take, whether it's defusing from a painful thought, making room for difficult emotions, or taking action aligned with your values, contributes to a more resilient and fulfilling life. Remember, the journey of healing and growth is ongoing, and each day is an opportunity to make progress.

Building a Support System for Ongoing Practice

Building a support system that encourages the ongoing practice of Trauma-Focused ACT (TF-ACT) principles is an essential component of your journey toward healing and living a fulfilling life. When you surround yourself with individuals who understand and support your efforts, you create a safety net that helps you navigate the challenges that inevitably arise. This network can be composed of friends, family, and professionals who share your commitment to psychological flexibility and personal growth.

Finding supportive friends and family members can sometimes feel like a daunting task, especially if your trauma has led to feelings of isolation or mistrust. Start by reaching out to those who have shown empathy and understanding in the past. These individuals might be close friends, family members, or even acquaintances who have demonstrated a willingness to listen and provide a supportive ear. Share your journey with them, explaining the principles of TF-ACT and how they are helping you manage your thoughts and emotions. When you open up about your experiences, you create an opportunity for deeper connection and mutual support.

Professional help is another crucial aspect of building a robust support system. Therapists, counselors, and coaches who specialize in trauma and ACT can provide expert guidance and a safe space to explore your feelings and challenges. They can offer strategies and techniques that you might not have encountered on your own, and they can help you stay accountable to your goals. Consider joining support groups or online communities where you can connect with others who are on similar paths. These groups can be a source of encouragement, practical advice, and a sense of belonging.

During challenging times, it's easy to fall into the trap of isolation and self-doubt. However, leaning on your support system can make all the difference. When you feel overwhelmed, reach out to a trusted friend, family member, or therapist. Share your struggles and successes, and allow them to offer their perspectives and encouragement. Remember that asking for help is a sign of strength, not weakness. It shows that you are committed to your well-being and are willing to take the necessary steps to maintain your mental health.

Creating a supportive environment also involves setting boundaries and communicating your needs clearly. Let your support system know what kind of help you need, whether it's a listening ear, a distraction, or practical assistance. Be open about your boundaries and what triggers might affect you. This transparency helps your support system understand how to best support you and can prevent misunderstandings or unintentional harm.

Incorporating TF-ACT principles into your daily life is a gradual process, and having a supportive network can make this journey more manageable and rewarding. Your support system can help you stay motivated, provide new insights, and celebrate your progress. By fostering these connections, you build a community that not only helps you navigate the challenges of trauma but also enriches your life with deeper relationships and a sense of purpose.

Maintaining Long-Term Motivation and Growth

Maintaining long-term motivation for personal growth is a critical aspect of trauma recovery, and Acceptance and Commitment Therapy (ACT) offers a wealth of principles to guide you on this journey. Imagine your recovery as a river, continuously flowing and adapting to the landscape it encounters. Just as a river finds its path around obstacles, you too can navigate the challenges of your healing process with resilience and determination.

One of the core principles of ACT is values-based living. Your values are the compass that guides your actions and decisions. To maintain motivation, it's essential to reconnect with your deepest values regularly. Spend some time reflecting on what truly matters to you. Is it family, creativity, personal growth, or contributing to your community? Once you have a clear understanding of your values, you can set goals that align with them. These goals become the milestones on your journey, giving you a sense of direction and purpose.

Setting new goals is a dynamic process. Instead of setting one large, overwhelming goal, break it down into smaller, manageable steps. For example, if your value is personal growth, a large goal might be to complete a degree. Break this down into smaller goals like attending a workshop, reading a book on the subject, or joining a study group. Each small step you take is a victory, and celebrating these small wins is crucial. When you achieve a small goal, take a moment to acknowledge your progress. This could be as simple as treating yourself to a favorite meal, sharing your success with a friend, or writing a journal entry about your accomplishment. Celebrating these moments reinforces your motivation and builds momentum.

Tracking your progress is another powerful tool. Keep a journal or a digital log to document your journey. Write about the steps you've taken, the challenges you've faced, and the insights you've gained. Reflecting on your progress can provide a sense of accomplishment and help you stay focused on your long-term goals. It's also a way to see how far you've come, which can be incredibly motivating during difficult times.

In the spirit of ACT, mindfulness is a practice that can greatly enhance your motivation. Mindfulness involves being present and fully engaged in the moment. When you practice mindfulness, you become more aware of your thoughts and emotions, allowing you to respond to them with greater clarity and intention. This can help you stay grounded and focused on your goals, even when faced with setbacks. Try incorporating mindfulness practices into your daily routine, such as meditation, deep breathing exercises, or mindful walking. These practices can help you stay centered and connected to your values.

Another strategy is to build a support network. Recovery is a journey that is often easier with the help of others. Surround yourself with people who understand and support your goals. This could be friends, family, a therapist, or a support group. Share your progress with them, and don't hesitate to ask for encouragement or advice when you need it. A supportive community can provide the emotional boost you need to stay motivated.

Lastly, remember that recovery is not a linear process. There will be ups and downs, and it's important to be kind to yourself during these times. When you encounter setbacks, view them as opportunities to learn and grow. Use the principles of ACT to accept the challenges and commit to moving forward. Your journey is unique, and the most important thing is to keep moving in the direction of your values.

By integrating these strategies into your daily life, you can maintain the motivation needed to continue your healing journey. Each step you take, no matter how small, is a step toward a more fulfilling and meaningful life. Keep your values at the forefront of your mind, celebrate your progress, and stay committed to the path of personal growth. Your journey is a testament to your strength and resilience, and with each step, you are reclaiming control of your life.

Navigating Setbacks with ACT Tools

As you navigate through the process of integrating Trauma-Focused Acceptance and Commitment Therapy (TF-ACT) into your daily life, it's important to be prepared for the inevitable setbacks. These challenges are not signs of failure but rather natural parts of the healing and growth process. Embracing this perspective can transform your relationship with difficulties, making them stepping stones rather than stumbling blocks.

Mindfulness is a powerful tool that can help you navigate these moments with grace and resilience. When a setback occurs, take a moment to pause and breathe. Allow yourself to fully experience the present moment, without judgment. Notice the sensations in your body, the sounds around you, and the thoughts that arise. By practicing mindfulness, you create a space between your experiences and your reactions, giving you the clarity to choose how you want to respond. This can be particularly helpful when old patterns of thinking or reacting start to surface. Instead of automatically falling into those patterns, you can observe them with curiosity and compassion, understanding that they are just part of your journey.

Cognitive defusion is another essential technique that can help you manage challenging thoughts. When you encounter a setback, it's common for negative thoughts to flood your mind. These thoughts might tell you that you're not good enough, that you'll never overcome your trauma, or that you should give up. Instead of believing these thoughts, try to see them for what they are: just words and images that your mind generates. You can use techniques like labeling (e.g., "This is just a thought about failure") or distancing (e.g., "I notice I'm having the thought that I can't do this"). By defusing from these thoughts, you can prevent them from controlling your actions and emotions. This doesn't mean you ignore your feelings; rather, you acknowledge them and choose to act in alignment with your values, even if it feels difficult.

Values-based action is the cornerstone of TF-ACT, and it becomes especially crucial during setbacks. When you encounter a challenge, take a moment to reconnect with your core values. Ask yourself, "What is truly important to me in this moment?" and "What action can I take that aligns with these values, even if it's a small step?" For example, if your value is to build meaningful relationships, you might decide to reach out to a friend for support, even if you feel vulnerable. If your value is to live a healthy lifestyle, you might choose to take a walk or practice a relaxation technique, even if you're feeling overwhelmed. By acting in accordance with your values, you reinforce your commitment to the life you want to live, regardless of the obstacles you face.

It's also important to practice self-compassion during tough moments. Be kind to yourself, just as you would be to a dear friend. Acknowledge that setbacks are a normal part of the healing process and that everyone experiences them. Instead of beating yourself up, offer yourself words of encouragement and understanding. You might say, "It's okay to feel this way. I'm doing the best I can, and I will keep moving forward." This self-compassionate approach can help you maintain your resilience and motivation, even when things get tough.

Remember, the path to healing and growth is not linear. There will be ups and downs, and that's perfectly okay. Each setback is an opportunity to learn more about yourself, to deepen your practice of TF-ACT, and to move closer to the life you envision. By using mindfulness, cognitive defusion, and values-based action, you can transform setbacks into valuable lessons and continue to make meaningful progress. You are capable of navigating these challenges, and with each step, you are regaining control of your life and creating a future filled with purpose and fulfillment.

Living a Life of Meaning and Purpose After Trauma

As you delve deeper into the principles of Trauma-Focused ACT, it becomes increasingly clear that the path to a life filled with meaning and purpose is not just a distant dream but a tangible reality. The journey of integrating these principles into your daily life is a transformative one, filled with moments of growth, resilience, and profound change. Let's explore how fully embracing ACT can lead to a life that is not only manageable but deeply fulfilling, even in the wake of trauma.

Consider the story of Sarah, a woman who had experienced a series of traumatic events that left her feeling lost and disconnected from the world around her. For years, she struggled with intrusive thoughts, anxiety, and a profound sense of helplessness. It was only after she began to explore Trauma-Focused ACT that she started to see a glimmer of hope. Through the practice of mindfulness, Sarah learned to observe her thoughts and emotions without judgment, allowing her to create some much-needed distance from the pain that had once defined her. She began to engage in values-based actions, small steps that aligned with what truly mattered to her, such as reconnecting with her family and pursuing her passion for art. Over time, these actions became a part of her daily life, and she found that the more she lived in alignment with her values, the more meaning and purpose she discovered.

Another inspiring example is John, a veteran who had returned from deployment with deep emotional scars. His trauma had left him feeling isolated and numb, and he struggled to find a sense of belonging or purpose in civilian life. Through Trauma-Focused ACT, John learned to accept his past without letting it dictate his present. He practiced self-compassion and began to see himself with the same kindness and understanding he would offer to a friend. John started volunteering at a local veterans' support group, where he found a community of people who understood his struggles. This sense of connection and purpose became a cornerstone of his recovery, and he now speaks at events, sharing his story to inspire others who are on similar journeys.

These stories are not just isolated cases; they are testaments to the power of Trauma-Focused ACT. By fully integrating these principles into your daily life, you too can transform your relationship with trauma and find a path forward that is rich with meaning and purpose. The key lies in the consistent practice of mindfulness, acceptance, and values-based living. Each small step you take, whether it's a moment of mindful breathing, a compassionate self-talk, or an action that aligns with your values, contributes to a larger tapestry of healing and growth.

Embracing Trauma-Focused ACT is about more than just managing pain; it's about living a life that is deeply connected to what truly matters to you. It's about finding the courage to face your past, the strength to live in the present, and the hope to look forward to a future filled with possibilities. As you continue on this journey, remember that you are not alone. The principles of ACT are there to guide you, and the stories of those who have walked this path before you serve as a beacon of hope and resilience. With each step, you are reclaiming your life, one moment at a time.

Conclusion

Maintain Lasting Healing and Growth

"Trauma is not what happens to us, but what we hold inside in the absence of an empathetic witness."
Peter A. Levine

As we reach the conclusion of this journey through Trauma-Focused Acceptance and Commitment Therapy (TF-ACT), it is essential to reflect on the transformative power of the principles we have explored. The path to healing from trauma is not a linear one, but rather a winding road that requires ongoing commitment, self-compassion, and a willingness to embrace the present moment. This final chapter is dedicated to empowering you to maintain and deepen the healing and growth you have already achieved, ensuring that the principles of TF-ACT continue to guide you toward a more fulfilling and meaningful life.

Throughout this book, we have delved into the core principles of ACT and how they can be adapted to address the unique challenges of trauma. We have explored the importance of acceptance, mindfulness, values, committed action, and cognitive defusion. Each of these principles serves as a tool in your toolkit, helping you to navigate the complex emotions and thoughts that often accompany trauma. By integrating these tools into your daily life, you can build a foundation of psychological flexibility that allows you to face life's challenges with resilience and grace.

One of the most profound lessons of TF-ACT is the concept of acceptance. Acceptance does not mean resignation or giving up; rather, it is about acknowledging the reality of your experiences and emotions without judgment. This acceptance is a crucial first step in the healing process, as it allows you to release the grip of avoidance and denial. By accepting your past, you free yourself to focus on the present and the future. This does not mean that painful memories will disappear, but it does mean that you can coexist with them in a way that no longer controls your life.

Mindfulness, another cornerstone of TF-ACT, is the practice of being fully present in the moment. It involves observing your thoughts and feelings without getting entangled in them. By cultivating mindfulness, you can develop a greater awareness of your internal and external experiences, allowing you to respond to them with intention rather than reactivity. This practice can be particularly powerful for those who have experienced trauma, as it helps to break the cycle of rumination and hyperarousal that often accompanies traumatic memories.

Values play a crucial role in guiding your actions and decisions. By identifying and connecting with your core values, you can create a sense of purpose and direction that transcends the pain of your past. Values are the compass that guides you toward a life that is meaningful and fulfilling. They provide a framework for making choices that align with who you want to be and what you want to achieve. When you act in accordance with your values, you build a life that is rich and rewarding, regardless of the challenges you face.

Committed action is the bridge between your values and your actions. It involves taking concrete steps to live in a way that is consistent with your values, even when it is difficult. This might mean setting boundaries, seeking support, or pursuing new opportunities. Committed action is about making a commitment to yourself to live a life that is true to your deepest desires and aspirations. It is about taking small, consistent steps that lead to significant changes over time.

Cognitive defusion is a powerful technique for gaining distance from unhelpful thoughts and beliefs. By learning to observe your thoughts without getting caught up in them, you can reduce their impact on your emotional well-being. This skill is particularly useful for managing the intrusive thoughts and negative self-talk that often accompany trauma. By defusing from these thoughts, you can create a mental space that allows you to respond to your experiences with clarity and calm.

As you move forward, it is important to recognize that the journey of healing and growth is ongoing. Trauma recovery is not a destination but a process. There will be moments of progress and moments of setback, and that is perfectly normal. The key is to approach this process with self-compassion and a growth mindset. Be gentle with yourself when you encounter challenges, and celebrate your successes, no matter how small they may seem. Each step you take, no matter how minor, is a step toward a more resilient and fulfilling life.

To maintain and deepen your healing, consider the following strategies:

1. **Regular Practice**: Incorporate mindfulness and other TF-ACT practices into your daily routine. Just as physical exercise strengthens your body, regular mental and emotional practices will strengthen your psychological flexibility.

2. **Seek Support**: Continue to seek support from trusted friends, family, or mental health professionals. Having a supportive network can provide the encouragement and guidance you need to stay on track.

3. **Reflect on Progress**: Take time to reflect on your journey and the progress you have made. Celebrate your achievements and learn from your setbacks. This reflection can help you stay motivated and focused on your goals.

4. **Stay Connected to Your Values**: Regularly revisit your core values and ensure that your actions align with them. This connection can provide a sense of purpose and direction, even in challenging times.

5. **Embrace New Challenges**: Be open to new experiences and opportunities. Growth often comes from stepping out of your comfort zone and embracing the unknown.

In conclusion, the principles of TF-ACT offer a powerful framework for managing the painful thoughts and experiences that can arise from trauma. By integrating these principles into your daily life, you can build a foundation of psychological flexibility that allows you to live a more fulfilling and meaningful life. Remember, the journey of healing and growth is a lifelong process, and you have the potential to continue evolving and thriving. Trust in your resilience, and know that you have the tools and support to navigate whatever challenges come your way. With each step, you are moving closer to a life that is true to your values and filled with purpose and joy.